Denise Marchini
Hugh Boyde

Business English for Beginners

Workbook

Cornelsen & OXFORD

Verfasserin/Verfasser	Denise Marchini, Bern; Hugh Boyde, Cambridge
Berater	Anthony Fitzpatrick, Frankfurt; Crayton Walker, ISD, Stuttgart
Außenredaktion	Context Englischsprachige Medien, Bad Münstereifel
Gestaltung und Herstellung	Marc Berger
Zeichnungen	David Graham S. 16 Kim Lane S. 19, 24, 25, 30, 54 Duncan Smith S. 11, 21, 22, 30, 32, 48, 54, 62, 73

1. Auflage

5.	4.	3.	2.	1.
1998	97	96	95	94

Alle Drucke dieser Auflage können, weil untereinander unverändert, im Unterricht nebeneinander verwendet werden.

Bestellnummer **22528**
ISBN 3-8109-2252-8

Druck und *Weiterverarbeitung* Saladruck, Berlin
Vertrieb Cornelsen Verlag, Berlin

Gedruckt auf Recyclingpapier, hergestellt aus 100% Altpapier.

Inhalt

Hinweise an den Benutzer

Dieses Workbook enthält zusätzliches Übungsmaterial, das Sie alleine zu Hause bearbeiten können. Der Schlüssel zu allen Übungen befindet sich im Anhang.
Die Units des Workbook entsprechen denen des Student's Book. Zusätzlich finden Sie am Anfang des Workbook - auf den hier unmittelbar folgenden Seiten - eine Nullunit, die als Vorbereitung auf die Arbeit mit Business English for Beginners gedacht ist. Einige sehr einfache Grammatikstrukturen, die Grundzahlen 1-1000 und die englischen Namen der Wochentage und Monate werden vorgestellt und geübt.
Wenn Sie schon irgendwann einmal Englisch gelernt haben, können Sie dieses grundlegende Sprachmaterial anhand der Unit 0 wiederholen und festigen. Wenn Sie noch nie Englisch gelernt haben, empfiehlt es sich auf jeden Fall die Unit 0 vorab zu bearbeiten, damit Sie sich den Einstieg in die ersten Stunden erleichtern.

The Sales Department

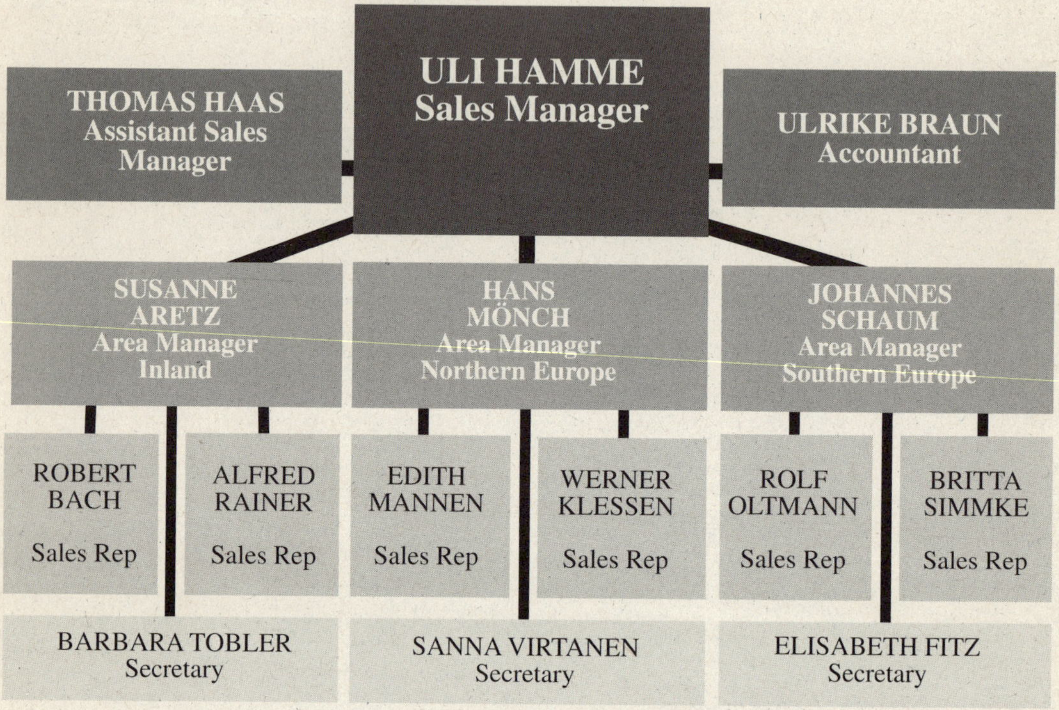

sales = Verkaufs-; department = Abteilung; manager = Leiter/in; assistant = stellvertretend; accountant = Buchhalter/in; area = Gebiet; sales rep = Verkaufsvertreter/in; secretary = Sekretär/in; Northern/Southern Europe = Nord-/Südeuropa

to be

I am	ich bin	we are	wir sind
you are	du bist/Sie sind	you are	ihr seid/Sie sind
he is	er ist	they are	sie sind
she is	sie ist		
it is	es ist		

the, a, an

- **the** Bestimmter Artikel, Singular und Plural (der, die/das)
  Uli Hamme is the sales manager.
  Susanne, Hans, and Johannes are the area managers.
- **a** Unbestimmter Artikel vor einem Konsonanten (steht im Englischen auch vor Berufsangaben) (ein/eine)
  Barbara is a secretary.
- **an** Unbestimmter Artikel vor einem Vokal (ein/eine)
  Hans is an area manager.

1 Vervollständigen Sie mit 'a', 'an', 'the'.

1 Thomas Haas is ___________ assistant sales manager.

2 Sanna Virtanten is ___________ secretary.

3 Edith Mannen is ___________ sales rep.

4 Susanne Aretz, Hans Mönch and Johannes Schaum are ___________ area managers.

5 Ulrike Braun is ___________ accountant.

6 Hans Mönch is ___________ area manager.

7 Johannes Schaum is ___________ Southern Europe area manager.

8 Edith Mannen and Werner Klessen are ___________ Northern Europe sales reps.

9 Robert Bach and Alfred Rainer are ___________ inland sales reps.

10 Susanne Aretz is ___________ inland area manager.

2 Vervollständigen Sie mit einer Form von 'to be'.

1 Hello, I ___________ Johannes Schaum. I ___________ the Southern Europe area manager.

2 It ___________ a good sales department.

3 Susanne ___________ an area manager. She ___________ the inland area manager.

4 Susanne, Hans and Johannes ___________ the area managers. They ___________ in a meeting.

5 ___________ you a secretary?

6 Thomas Haas ___________ the assistant sales manager. He ___________ in a meeting.

7 We ___________ in the sales department. We ___________ sales reps.

8 ___________ you the inland area manager?

good = gut; meeting = Sitzung

Unit 0

Die Mehrzahl von Hauptwörtern

	Singular	Plural
	<u>regelmäßige Pluralbildung</u>	
	accountant	accountants (+s)
	manager	managers (+s)
	department	departments (+s)
	rep	reps (+s)
	office	offices (+s)
	boss	bosses (+es)
	secretary	secretaries (y = i+es)
	<u>unregelmäßige Pluralbildung</u>	
	man	men
	woman	women
	person	people

office = Büro; boss = Vorgesetzte/r; man = Mann; woman = Frau; person = Person

3 Bilden Sie den Plural.

1 one office, two ____________________

2 one salesperson, two ____________________

3 one secretary, two ____________________

4 one boss, two ____________________

5 one saleswoman, two ____________________

6 one meeting, two ____________________

7 one area, two ____________________

Die Possessivpronomen und das Genetiv-s

I am Thomas Haas. This is	my	office.
Is Sanna Virtanen	your	secretary?
He is Hans Mönch. Hamburg is in	his	sales area.
She is Susanne Aretz. Uli Hamme is	her	boss.
IBM is big.	Its	centre is in America.
We are sales reps. Susanne Aretz is	our	area manager.
Edith and Werner, is Hans Mönch	your	boss?
Rolf and Britta are reps. Johannes Schaum is	their	boss.
Sanna Virtanen is	Hans Mönch's	secretary.
Uli Hamme is	Thomas Haas'	boss.

big = groß

4 **Ergänzen Sie.**

1 The sales department is big. __________ boss is Uli Hamme.

2 I am Britta Simmke. __________ area manager is Johannes Schaum.

3 Robert Bach and I are sales reps. Susanne Aretz is __________ area manager.

4 Johannes __________ secretary is Elisabeth Fitz.

5 Thomas __________ boss is Uli Hamme.

6 Hello, Mr Hamme. Is Thomas Haas __________ assistant manager?

7 Robert and Alfred, is Susanne Aretz __________ area manager?

8 Uli Hamme is the sales manager. __________ assistant manager is Thomas Haas.

9 Susanne Aretz is an area manager. Robert Bach and Alfred Rainer are __________ sales reps.

10 Rolf Oltmann and Britta Simmke are sales reps. __________ area manager is Johannes Schaum.

Die Zahlen

0	zero		
1	one	21	twenty-one
2	two	22	twenty-two
3	three	23	twenty-three
4	four	24	twenty-four
5	five	25	twenty-five
6	six	26	twenty-six
7	seven	27	twenty-seven
8	eight	28	twenty-eight
9	nine	29	twenty-nine
10	ten	30	thirty
11	eleven		
12	twelve	40	forty
13	thirteen	50	fifty
14	fourteen	60	sixty
15	fifteen	70	seventy
16	sixteen	80	eighty
17	seventeen	90	ninety
18	eighteen	100	one hundred
19	nineteen		
20	twenty	1,000	one thousand

Unit 0

5 Schreiben Sie die Rechenaufgaben.

Beispiel 13 + 6 = Thirteen and six is nineteen.

1 2 + 28 =

2 500 + 300 + 200 =

3 95 + 4 =

4 10 + 5 + 13 =

5 22 + 55 =

6 8 + 17 + 29 =

7 15 + 11 + 14 =

Die Uhrzeit

10.00	ten o'clock / ten a.m.
22.00	ten o'clock / ten p.m.
9.15	a quarter past nine / nine fifteen (a.m.)
21.15	a quarter past nine / nine fifteen (p.m.)
11.30	half past eleven / eleven thirty (a.m.)
7.45	a quarter to eight / seven forty-five (a.m.)
19.45	a quarter to eight / seven forty-five (p.m.)

a.m. = 00.01 - 12.00 p.m. = 12.01 - 24.00

Die Wochentage

Monday, Tuesday, Wednesday, Thursday, Friday, Saturday, Sunday

with, at, on, in, to, from

a meeting	with Uli	at eight o'clock/a.m.	on Monday
a meeting	in Rome	at eleven thirty (a.m.)	on Wednesday
a flight	to Rome	at eight fifteen (a.m.)	on Wednesday
a flight	from Rome	at three forty-five (p.m.)	on Friday

with = mit; at = um; on = am; in = in; flight = Flug; to = nach; from = aus

6 Annas Woche.

21 Monday	22 Tuesday	23 Wednesday	24 Thursday	25 Friday	26 Saturday	27 Sunday
8 a.m. meeting	2 p.m. meeting	8.15 a.m.				
with Uli	in the	flight to		3.45 p.m.		4 p.m.
10 a.m. telephone	conference room	Rome		flight from	1 p.m.	meeting
conference			9 p.m. jazz	Rome	lunch with	with
11 a.m. meeting	8 p.m. dinner	11.30 a.m.	concert		Sylvia	Lorenzo
with T. Haas	at Lorenzini's	meeting				
8.15 p.m. opera	restaurant	in Rome				
in Berne						

March week 12 199-

opera = Oper; dinner = Abendessen; concert = Konzert; lunch = Mittagessen; What time? = Um wieviel Uhr?

Beantworten Sie die Fragen.

Beispiel What time is the opera in Berne on Monday?
It's (It is) at eight fifteen p.m.

1 What time is Anna's lunch with Sylvia on Saturday?

____

2 What time is Anna's meeting in Rome on Wednesday?

____

3 What time is the jazz concert on Thursday?

____

4 What time is the telephone conference on Monday?

____

5 What time is Anna's meeting with Thomas Haas on Monday?

____

Ergänzen Sie.

6 Anna's meeting _______ the conference room is _______ Tuesday _______ 2.00 p.m.

7 Her flight _______ Rome is _______ 8.15 a.m. _______ Wednesday.

8 Her dinner _______ Lorenzini's restaurant is _______ 8.00 p.m. _______ Tuesday.

9 Her meeting with Lorenzo is _______ Sunday _______ 4 p.m.

10 Her flight _______ Rome is _______ 3.45 p.m. _______ Friday.

Unit 0

Die Monate

January, February, March, April, May, June, July, August, September, October, November, December

7 **Das Jahr von Sabine Loew. Ergänzen Sie die Sätze.**

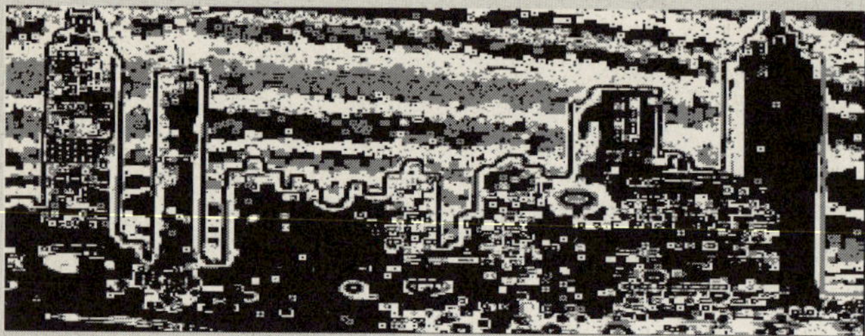

JANUARY

Mon	Tue	Wed	Thur	Fri	Sat	Sun
	1	2	3	4	5	6
7	8	9	10	11	12	13
14	15	16	17	18	19	20
21	22	23	24	25	26	27
28	29	30	31			

Looking ahead

holiday in Zermatt	3.2 - 15.2
conference in Rome	2.3.- 5.3
computer course	25.5 - 28.5
meeting in Bonn	5.6 - 6.6
birthday!	7.7
holiday in France	3.8 - 17.8
English course	
in London	10.10 - 16.10
conference in Munich	4.11 - 6.11

holiday = Urlaub; course = Kurs; birthday = Geburtstag; France = Frankreich

1 Sabine Loew's holiday in Zermatt is in ____________________.

2 Her meeting in Bonn is in ____________________.

3 Her computer course is in ____________________.

4 Her holiday in France is in ____________________.

5 Her English course in London is in ____________________.

6 Her birthday is in ____________________.

7 Her conference in Munich is in ____________________.

Was haben Sie in den kommenden 12 Monaten vor?
Beispiel My holiday is in August.

Unit 1

1 **Lesen Sie 'Welcome to Interbit!', SB Seite 5.**
True or False? Richtig oder Falsch? (→ SB 4)

		True	False
1	Dieter is busy.	❍	❍
2	Dieter is fine.	❍	❍
3	Sue Bishop is from New York.	❍	❍
4	The meeting is in New York.	❍	❍
5	Sabine is a software expert.	❍	❍
6	Dieter Hennings is from Berlin.	❍	❍
7	Richard, Dieter and Sabine are at IBM .	❍	❍
8	Dieter is the sales manager.	❍	❍

2 **To be. Ergänzen Sie.** (→ SB 5)

Clara Messner,
saleswoman,
Konstanz

Heinz Dietrich,
accountant,
Berlin

Anna Bornmann,
software engineer
Berlin

Janet and Philip Aston
engineers,
Oxford

1 Hello, I'm Heinz Dietrich. __________ an accountant.

2 I __________ Anna Bornmann. __________ a software engineer.

3 Hello, I __________ Clara Messner. __________ a saleswoman.

4 This __________ Heinz Dietrich. __________ an accountant.

5 This __________ Anna Bornmann. __________ a software engineer.

6 Clara __________ a saleswoman and Heinz __________ an accountant.

7 I'm Heinz Dietrich. I __________ from Berlin and this __________ Clara Messner.

8 Hello. I'm Janet Aston and this __________ Philip Aston. We __________ from Oxford.

9 Janet and Philip __________ English. __________ technicians.

10 Anna and Heinz __________ from Berlin. Where __________ you from?

3 **Ergänzen Sie diesen Dialog.** (→ SB 4)

Clara Hi, Heinz! How are you?

Heinz Clara! Hello! ____________________, and you?

Clara ____________________, thank you. ____________________ you here for the meeting at 11.00?

Heinz ____________________ right. ____________________ is the meeting?

Clara ____________________ in Room 35.

Heinz ____________________ we far?

Clara No, ____________________ not far.

4 **Sich begrüßen. Übersetzen Sie.** (→ SB 4)

1 Hallo, Dieter! Wie geht es dir?

____

2 Danke, gut. Und dir?

____

3 Frau Baumgartner, darf ich Uwe Heckendorn vorstellen?

____

4 Uwe, darf ich Frau Baumgartner vorstellen?

____

5 Es freut mich, Sie kennenzulernen.

____

6 Sehr erfreut.

____

5 **Fragen und Kurzantworten. Schreiben Sie.** (→ SB 8)

Beispiel Dieter/sales manager? (Yes)
Is Dieter a sales manager? - Yes, he is.

1 Sue/software expert? (Yes)

____

____

2 this/the conference room? (No)

____

____

3 Richard/from London? (No)

____

____

4 the salesmen/here? (No)

____

____

5 you/English student? (Yes)

____

____

6 I/right? (No)

____

____

6 **Übersetzen Sie.** (→ SB 8)

Ihr Chef, Herr Atkinson, spricht nur Englisch. Er ist mit Herrn Kaiser verabredet.
Die Sekretärin Herrn Kaisers, Susanne Fitz, kann sehr wenig Englisch.
Sie sind Dolmetscher/in.

SF = Susanne Fitz, RA = Richard Atkinson

SF Sind Sie der Chefingenieur?

You ______________________________

RA That's right. I'm here for a meeting with Mr Kaiser. Is the meeting at 10.00 o'clock?

You ______________________________

____

SF Ja, um 10 Uhr.

You ______________________________

RA And where is it?

You ______________________________

SF Hier, in diesem Zimmer.

You ______________________________

7 **Ergänzen Sie.** (→ SB 8)

1 ________________ Dieter from Hamburg? - No, ________________.

2 ________________ is he from? - ________________ from Augsburg.

3 And Sue? ________________ she from Augsburg, too? - No, ________________.
________________ from England.

4 ________________ you from Berlin? - No, we ________________.

5 ________________ you accountants? - Yes, ________________.

6 ________________ are you? - Fine, thanks, and you?

7 ________________ is the meeting? - In Room 15.

8 ________________ the meeting at 9 a.m.? - No, ________________.

9 ________________ is it? - ________________ at 10 o'clock.

10 ________________ is the sales manager? - Dieter Hennings is the sales manager.

11 ________________ Sue and Jutta software experts? - Yes, ________________.

12 ________________ this your computer? - No, ________________.

13 Whose computer ________________ this? - ________________ Dieter's computer.

14 ________________ things ________________ these? Are they your things? -
No, ________________.

8 **Bilden Sie Fragen.** (→ SB 8)

Beispiel Yes, they're my things.- Are these/those/they your things?

1 Yes, it's my computer.

____

2 No, they aren't our books.

____

3 This is Mr Henning's room.

____

4 The software expert's name is Sue.

____

5 No, I'm not. I'm free.

____

9 Wortschatz. Schreiben Sie die Wörter richtig hin.

1 (eewlcom) ____________________ to Interbit!

2 Hi, Dieter! Are you (eefr) ____________________?

3 (woh) ____________________ do you do.

4 (desaelp) ____________________ to meet you.

5 I'm an (ccttounnaa) ____________________.

6 Who is the managing (rotdirce) ____________________?

7 Can you (pells) ____________________ that, please?

8 The (haeqdaurerts) ____________________ of Interbit are in Berlin.

9 The meeting is in the conference (moor) ____________________.
We're not (raf) ____________________.

10 (eehrw) ____________________ is the conference room?

10 Wiederholung. Possessivpronomen und Genetiv-s. Ergänzen Sie.

Under 30

IFC GmbH, InfoAktuell and Funware Inc are all international companies with __________ headquarters in Germany. IFC__________ headquarters are in Frankfurt, InfoAktuell _____ headquarters are in Munich, and Funware__________ headquarters are in Berlin. They are all computer software companies and __________ managing directors are all under 30. IFC's managing director is 29, and __________ name is Peter Gutfeldt. InfoAktuell's managing director is 28, and __________ name is Susanne Wolf. Funware's managing director is only 24, and __________ name is J.R. Ewing!

Unit 2

branches	5	Munich	Berlin	Paris	Zurich	Vienna
telephonists	12	2	3	4	1	2
secretaries	213	46	56	54	25	32
receptionists	21	5	5	5	3	3
technicians	35	7	8	9	5	6
computer engineers	13	3	3	3	2	2
sales reps	17	5	4	4	2	2

1 Have got. Ergänzen Sie mit der richtigen Form. (→ SB 2)

Beispiel Tip Top has got 25 secretaries in Zurich.

1 Tip Top ________________ 17 sales reps in Europe.

2 They ________________ eight technicians in Vienna, they ________________ six.

3 The Berlin branch ________________ four sales reps, but it ________________ four telephonists.

4 The company ________________ three computer engineers in Paris and three in Zurich. It ________________ three in Paris, but it ________________ three in Zurich.

5 The branch in Munich ________________ 50 secretaries. It ________________ 46.

6 The Berlin and Paris branches ________________ five receptionists, the Zurich branch ________________ three.

2 **Have got: Fragen. Bilden Sie jeweils zwei Fragen.** (→ SB 2)

Beispiel the company/10 secretaries in Zurich
Has the company got 10 secretaries in Zurich?
How many secretaries has it got?

1 the company/three sales reps in Europe

____

____

2 the Berlin branch/four telephonists

____

____

3 they/seven technicians in Paris

____

____

4 the Berlin and Paris branches/four computer engineers

____

____

3 **Have got. Bilden Sie Sätze.** (→ SB 3)

Beispiel we, computer - fax
We've got a computer, but we haven't got a fax.

1 I, English-speaking secretary - German-speaking secretary

____

____

2 they, branch in Leipzig - van available in Leipzig

____

____

3 the van, fax - photocopier

____

4 Mrs Smythe, a big meeting - a secretary

____

____

4 **There is/are. Übersetzen Sie.** (→ SB 5)

1 Gibt es eine Filiale in Leipzig? - Ja, es gibt eine.

2 Gibt es Filialen in Frankreich? - Ja, es gibt zwei.

3 Gibt es Filialen in Irland? - Nein, es gibt keine.

4 Gibt es eine neue Filiale in München? - Nein, aber es gibt eine in Leipzig.

5 Gibt es zwei Computer in diesem Büro? - Nein, es gibt einen.

6 Gibt es ein Faxgerät in diesem Büro? - Ja, es gibt eins.

5 **Have got: Kurzantworten. Beantworten Sie.** (→ SB 6)

Beispiel Has Tip Top got three branches in Europe? – No, it hasn't.

1 Has Tip Top got 32 secretaries in Vienna?

2 Has the company got 25 receptionists?

3 Has the Berlin branch got five computer engineers?

4 Has it got five receptionists?

5 Have they got five sales reps in Munich?

6 Have they got five sales reps in Zurich?

7 Have the Munich and Vienna branches got two telephonists?

6 **Ortsangaben. Ergängen Sie mit 'in' (2x), 'to the north, across, to the west, to the east, near'.** (→ SB 10)

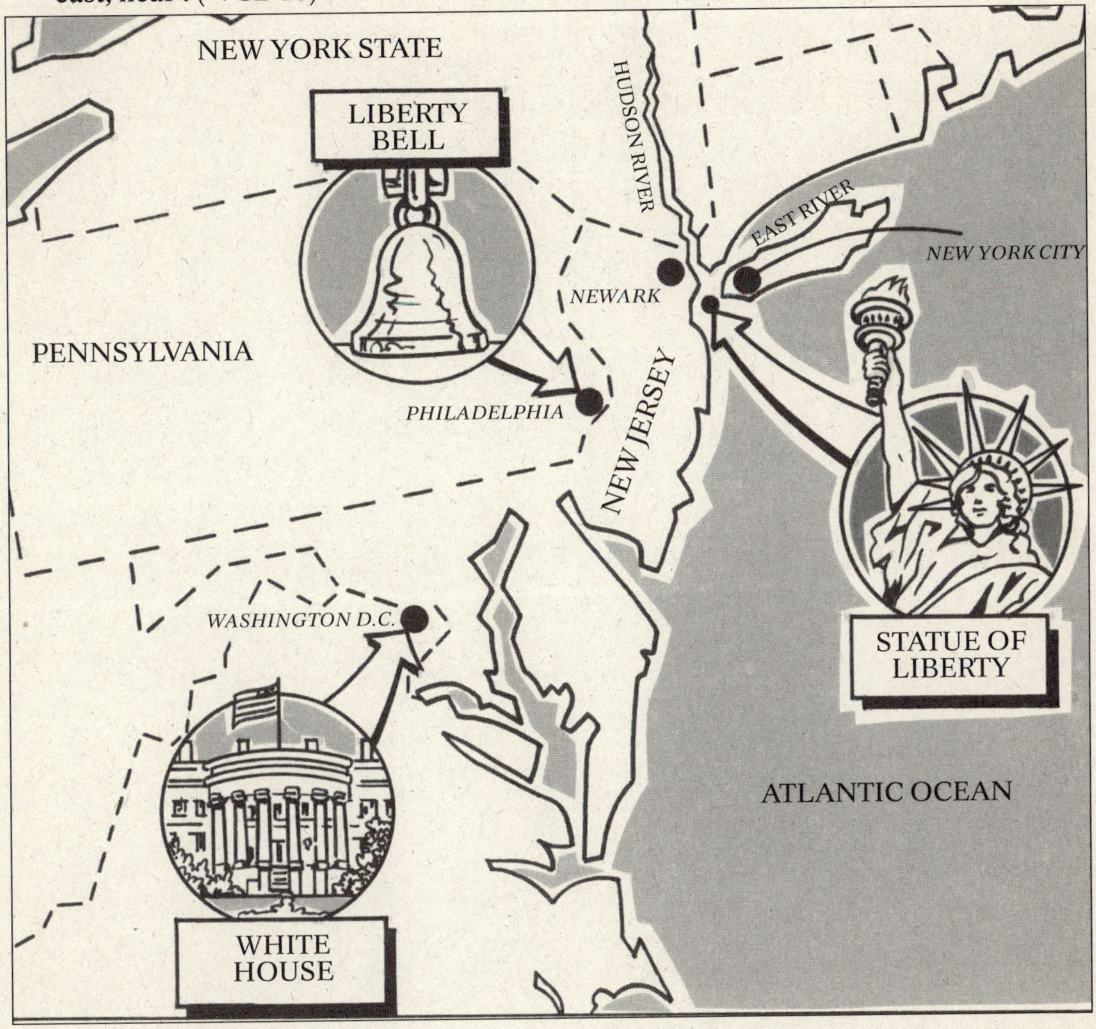

1 New York state is ______________________ of New Jersey.

2 The White House is ______________________ Washington D.C.

3 Newark is ______________________ of New York City.

4 New Jersey is ______________________ of Pennsylvania.

5 Philadelphia is ______________________ Pennsylvania.

6 New Jersey is ______________________ the Hudson River from New York City.

7 The Statue of Liberty isn't in New York City. It's ______________________ New York City.

Unit 2

7 **Wortschatz. Ergänzen Sie.** (→ SB 13)

1 Euroffice
They've got expert office ______________________ and modern office ______________________. They've got ten ______________________ in Europe.

2 In Paris
Jean Racine is the ______________________ of the Paris Euroffice branch. All of his ______________________ are booked tomorrow. One is at a big ______________________ near Newcastle.

3 In England
Carol Smythe is at the Euroffice ______________________ in England. She has got a van for the ______________________ outside Paris, where the Subitsi people are.

4 In Ashford
Mike O'Farrell and his ______________________ are near the Channel tunnel in Ashford. Their van is ______________________ for a week.

8 **Wiederholung: die Zahlen. Schreiben Sie die Zahlen aus**

	Berlin	Leipzig	London	Paris
Berlin	-	190	865	1070
Leipzig	190	-	845	970
London	865	845	-	415
Paris	1070	970	415	-

1 From Berlin to Leipzig is ______________________ kilometres.
2 From Paris to Leipzig is ______________________ kilometres.
3 From London to Paris is ______________________ kilometres.
4 From London to Berlin is ______________________ kilometres.
5 From Leipzig to London is ______________________ kilometres.

Unit 3

1 **Befehlen. Vervollständigen Sie diese verneinten Befehle mit 'Don't' und einem passenden Verb.** (→ SB 4)

1 ________________________ A3. Select A4.

2 ________________________ the 'Start' button until you put the originals on the feeder.

3 ________________________ the photocopier off.

4 ________________________ the originals after you make your copies.

5 ________________________ the front of the photocopier. Just kick it here, on the left!

6 ________________________ the red button.

2 **Bitten. Drücken Sie diese Befehle höflicher aus. Verwenden Sie 'please' mit den Wörtern in Klammern.** (→ SB 4)

Beispiel Check all the lights. (Would)
Would you please check all the lights?

1 Close the office for the weekend. (Can)

____

2 Check the computers. (Could)

____

3 Switch off the photocopier. (Can)

____

4 Put the key in my desk. (Would)

____

5 Tell me on Monday where it is. (Can)

____

6 Give David the keys. (Would)

____

7 Show me the letter. (Can)

____

8 Give me a pen. (Could)

____

Unit 3

3 **Objektpronomen. Ergänzen Sie mit dem richtigen Objektpronomen: me, you, him, her, it, us, them.** (→ SB 4)

1 Here is the paper. Put ______________ in the machine.

2 Have you got the originals? Good, now put ______________ in the feeder.

3 These are the engineers from Munich. Would you please show ______________ how the fax machine works?

4 I've got a problem with this computer. Can you tell ______________ how I switch ______________ on?

5 Have you got a problem? Can I help ______________?

6 Don't forget to find Sabine and to tell ______________ where the key is.

7 Richard, Mr Smith has got a problem with the video machine and I'm busy. Could you help ______________?

8 Christine! Joan and I have got a problem. Can you help ______________?

4 **Die einfache Form der Gegenwart. Ergänzen Sie.** (→ SB 8)

Beispiel __Does__ the paper go in here?
No, it __doesn't__.

1 ______________ you need a flipchart?

No, I ______________.

2 ______________ the green light mean the power is on?

Yes, it ______________.

3 ______________ the pause button always work?

No, it ______________.

4 ______________ I press the green button for rewind?

No, you ______________.

5 ______________ she check the fax machine at 9.00?

Yes, she ______________.

6 ______________ you all meet every morning?

No, we ______________.

5 **Die einfache Form der Gegenwart. Bilden Sie Sätze.** (→ SB 9)

Beispiel he/not often/fax us
He doesn't often fax us.

1 the machine/work like this

____

2 the machine/not/work without power

____

3 they/never/send originals

____

4 you/not always/need the overhead projector

____

5 the managers/never/meet before 4.30

____

6 **Adverbien der Häufigkeit Beantworten Sie die Fragen mit: always/usually/often/sometimes/rarely/never.** (→ SB 9)

Beispiel How often do you use a photocopier?
I never use a photocopier. *or* I often use a photocopier. *etc.*

1 How often do you work on Saturday?

____

2 How often do you use a computer?

____

3 How often do you use a video machine?

____

4 How often do you make phone calls to America?

____

5 How often do you use a telephone?

____

6 How often do you go to a conference?

____

7 **Bedienungsanweisungen. Korrigieren Sie den Text, indem Sie die kursiv gedruckten Wörte ändern. Beginnen Sie: 'First she puts...'.** (→ SB 10)

First ~~I put~~ she puts the originals into the feeder of my fax machine, like this. Then *I press* the "Dial" button[1] and then *I dial*[2] the number. Then *I wait* until the transmission[3] starts, because sometimes the line is engaged[4] and *I have* to[5] dial again. After the transmission, *I take* the originals and *file*[6] them.

[1] dial button = Wählknopf; [2] dial = wählen; [3] transmission = Übertragung; [4] engaged = besetzt ;
[5] have to = müssen; [6] file = ablegen

8 **Wortschatz. Benennen Sie diese Gegenstände.**

1 cassette player ______________________________

9 **Allgemeine Wiederholung. Ordnen Sie die Verben und Gegenstände einander zu.**

1 switch on ________ help
2 select ________ a phone call
3 need ___1___ the power
4 close ________ the phone
5 press ________ the door
6 make ________ a page size
7 pick up ________ a fax
8 send ________ the button

Unit 4

1 **Some /any. Stellen Sie und beantworten Sie Fragen.** (→ SB3)

SOBAKU CAR FACTORIES

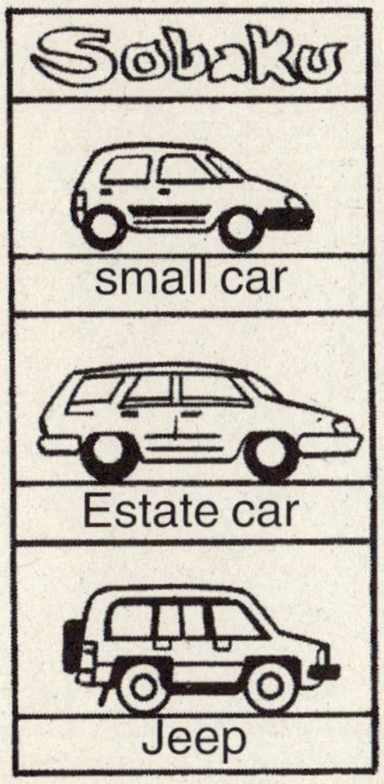

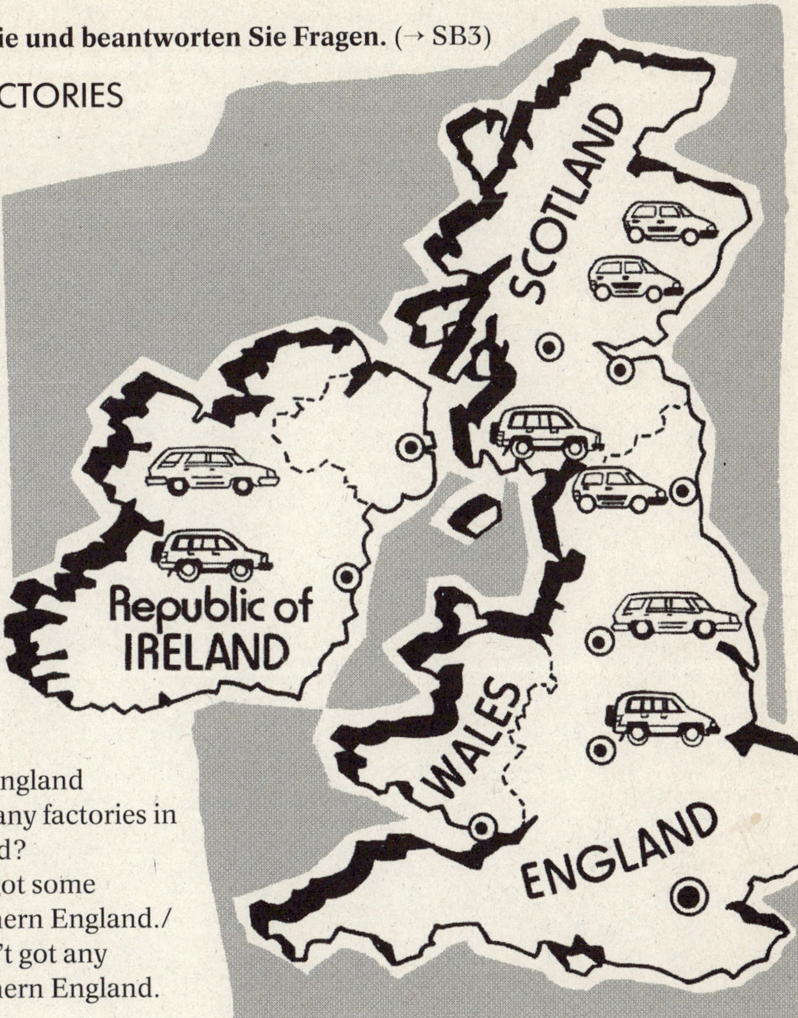

Example: southern England
Has Sobaku got any factories in southern England?
- Yes, they have got some factories in southern England./
No, they haven't got any factories in southern England.

1 northern England

____

____

2 Northern Ireland

____

____

3 the Republic of Ireland

____

____

Nun stellen Sie und beantworten Sie Fragen mit 'make'.

Beispiel: cars/the Republic of Ireland
Does Sobaku make any cars in the Republic of Ireland?
- Yes, they make some cars in the Republic of Ireland./
No, they don't make any cars in the Republic of Ireland.

4 small cars/Northern Ireland

____

____

5 estate cars/Scotland

____

____

6 cars/southern England

____

____

7 small cars/Wales

____

____

2 **Some/any/no/a. Ergänzen Sie.** (→ SB4)

1 Have you got __________ US dollars with you?

2 So, are there __________ questions?

3 No, I'm afraid we have got __________ staff available at the moment.

4 He has got __________ questions about the product.

5 The company employs __________ computer specialist, too.

6 No, I've got __________ dollars. But it's OK, I've got some marks.

7 I can't see __________ telephones here. Can you?

8 Do you employ __________ salespeople in England?

9 Have you got __________ staff available?

10 Have you got __________ programme?

11 I need __________ cables. Where are they?

12 Oh no! There is __________ paper in the photocopier.

13 We have got __________ problem with the new advertisement. – What, again?

14 Do you need __________ transparencies or photocopies for your presentation?

15 I have got __________ question.

3 **How much/How many. Bilden Sie Fragen.** (→ SB8)

Beispiel: employees/your company
How many employees are there in your company?

1 people/your office

____

2 Spanish/this book

____

3 discs/the desk

____

4 salt/that cheese

____

5 time/you got

____

6 equipment/in the van

____

7 copies/you need

____

8 meetings/you got next week

____

9 paper/the photocopier

____

10 working days/before the end of the month

____

4 **Much/many/a little/a few/a lot of. Ergänzen Sie.** (→SB8)

1 They have got ____________ problems with the new computer.
2 There are only ____________ people in his department.
3 They don't employ ____________ salespeople in Spain.
4 He has got ____________ meetings next week.
5 He hasn't got ____________ time next week.
6 There is ____________ information in the programme.
7 There aren't ____________ people at the meeting.
8 We do ____________ business in France.
9 No, I'm afraid there isn't ____________ software available for this computer.
10 He hasn't got ____________ questions.
11 She needs ____________ photocopies for her presentation.

5 **Allgemeine Wiederholung. Wie lautete die Frage?**

Beispiel
Antwort: Vans available now? Yes, I've got three.
Mögliche Frage: Have you got any vans available now?

1 Paper? No, I haven't got any.

____

2 Discs? Yes, I've got some in my desk.

____

3 Employees? They've got about 2000.

____

4 Factories? There are two in the south and two in the north.

____

5 Branches in France? Yes, they have got some – three or four, I think.

____

6 Wyoming? Yes, we've got some customers in Wyoming.

____

6 **Wortschatz. Ordnen Sie die richtigen Satzhälften einander zu.**

1 They don't produce much
2 She's responsible
3 He handles
4 We don't use much
5 We fill the jars
6 These products go

marmalade for the home market.
imported fruit in this factory.
for sales.
abroad.
with jam.
the administration.

1 ______________________________

2 ______________________________

3 ______________________________

4 ______________________________

5 ______________________________

6 ______________________________

7 **Allgemeine Wiederholung. Lesen Sie die Informationen und ergänzen Sie den Text.**

Mc Laren

McLaren Audio

Headquarters: Glasgow
Factories: Glasgow, Aberdeen, Edinburgh
Employees: 800
Products: audio goods, telecommunications equipment

Managing Director: Mr R. Bridges
Marketing Director: Mr F. Ward
Sales Manager (UK): Ms A. Stewart
Finance Director: Ms K. Lees
Sales Director: Ms L. Lethbridge
Sales Manager (Europe): Mr C. Bradley

McLaren Audio ________________ audio goods and telecommunications equipment. The company ________________ 800 people at its ________________ in Glasgow and its three ________________ in Scotland. The company ________________ its products in the UK and also in Europe. Ms Lethbridge is director of the sales ________________ and has two sales managers: Ms Stewart ________________ for the UK market and Mr Bradley ________________ European sales.

Test 1

Kreuzen Sie in diesem Test die jeweils richtige Lösung an. Für jede Aufgabe gibt es nur eine richtige Lösung.

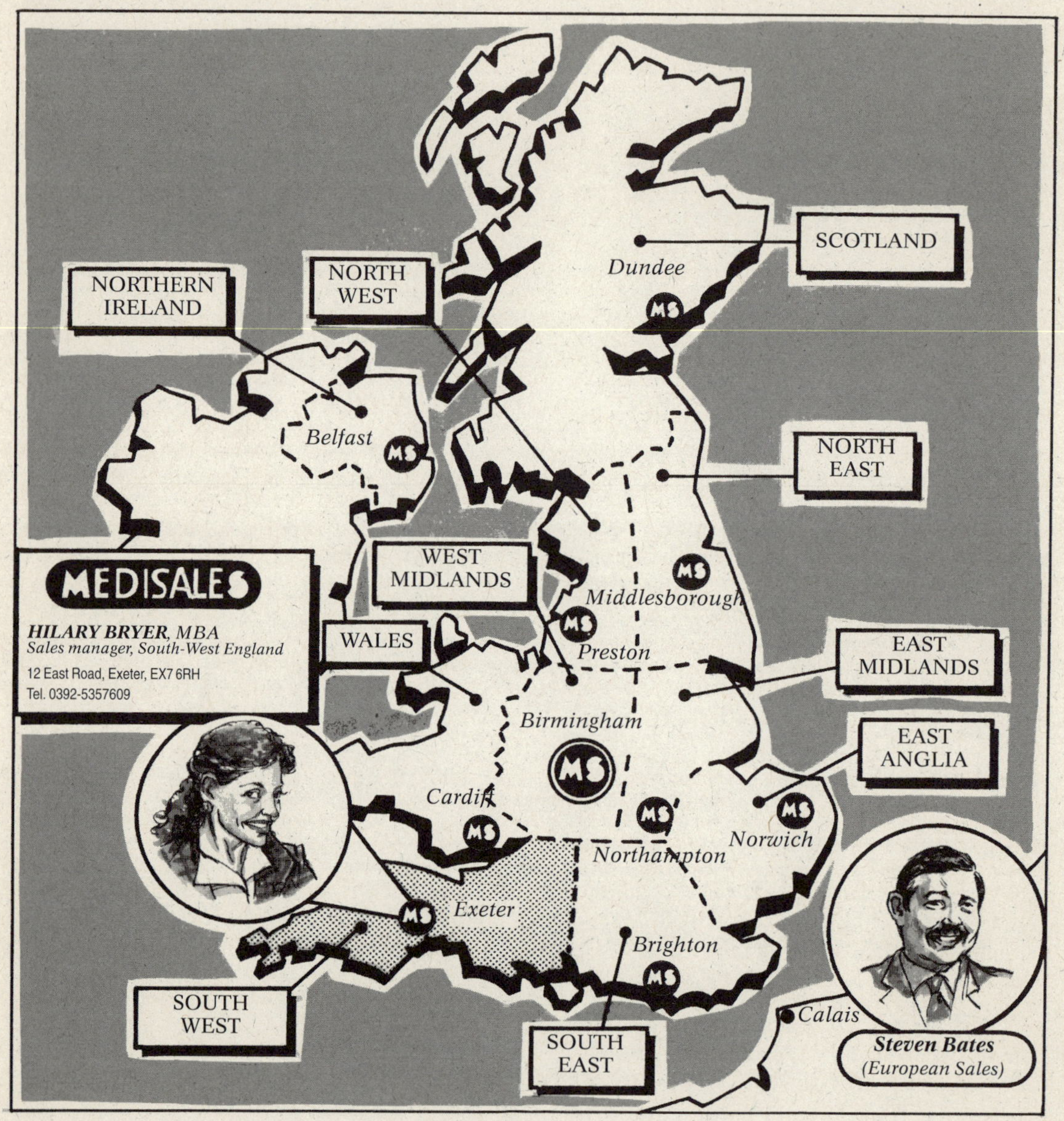

1 Grammatik

1 Hilary ... a sales manager.

- a am ❏
- b are ❏
- c is ❏
- d works ❏

2 ... 10 sales managers in the firm.

- a It has got ❏
- b There are ❏
- c There is ❏
- d They are ❏

3 Hilary ... work in South-East England.
- a aren't ❑
- b doesn't ❑
- c don't ❑
- d isn't ❑

4 Medisales has got an office in Northern Ireland, but it hasn't got ... salespeople in the Republic of Ireland.
- a a few ❑
- b any ❑
- c no ❑
- d some ❑

5 Is there a company office in Dundee?
- a Yes, it has. ❑
- b Yes, it is. ❑
- c Yes, there is. ❑
- d Yes, there's. ❑

6 ... an office in Exeter?
- a Does have the company ❑
- b Has got the company ❑
- c Has the company got ❑
- d Have got the company ❑

2 Wortschatz

1 Steven Bates ... export sales.
- a handles ❑
- b is ❑
- c responsible for ❑
- d works ❑

2 Steven often sees ... customers.
- a abroad ❑
- b foreign ❑
- c France ❑
- d outside ❑

3 Brighton is ... London.
- a in the south of ❑
- b southern ❑
- c southern of ❑
- d to the south of ❑

4 The company's ... are in Birmingham.
- a branches ❑
- b headquarters ❑
- c offices ❑
- d salespeople ❑

5 Steven Bates meets the people from the other offices every June. He sees ... at the sales conference.
- a the ❑
- b their ❑
- c them ❑
- d they ❑

3 Situationen

1 Bei einer Ausstellung wollen Sie von Hilary wissen, wie ein gewisses Gerät funktioniert. Sie fragen: 'Excuse me, ... show me this?'
- a could you ❑
- b don't ❑
- c do you ❑
- d have you got ❑

2 Nach der Erklärung bedanken Sie sich. Sie sagen 'Thank you.' Sie sagt: '...'.
- a Not at all. ❑
- b Nothing. ❑
- c Of course. ❑
- d Thanks. ❑

3 Jemand stellt Sie Stephen Bates vor. Er sagt: 'How do you do.' Sie sagen: '...'
- a Fine, thanks. ❑
- b How are you? ❑
- c How do you do. ❑
- d Pleased. ❑

4 Steven nennt Ihnen ein neues Produkt, dessen Name Sie sich notieren möchten. Sie fragen: '...'.
- a Can you spell that, please? ❑
- b How do you write, please? ❑
- c What's the name, please? ❑
- d You spell it, please. ❑

Unit 5

1 **Ordnungszahlen. Beantworten Sie.** (→ SB1)

Diese Arbeitskollegen übernachten heute im Heights Hotel in Birmingham. Sie gehen jetzt auf ihre Zimmer. Die erste Ziffer der Zimmernummer gibt das Stockwerk an. Fängt z.B. die Zimmernummer mit „5" an, so ist das Zimmer im 5. Stock. Das Hotel hat 12 Stockwerke.

Beispiel Which floor are you on, Mr Smith? (501)
- Well, my room number is 501, so I think I'm on the fifth floor.

1 Which floor are you on, Ms Nicholson?

____

2 Which floor are you on, Mr Carter?

____

3 What floor are you on, Mr Wright?

____

4 What floor are you on, Ms Jarvis?

____

5 What floor are you on Ms Anthony?

____

6 What floor are you on, Mr Shannon?

____

2 Indirekte Fragen. Stellen Sie Fragen mit 'Do you know ...'. (→ SB3)

Beispiel 1 Is there a photocopier here?
Do you know if there is a photocopier here?

1 Does he speak French?

2 Is he a specialist?

3 Is it with the other documents?

4 Have they got any staff available?

5 Do they export to the USA?

6 Are there any meeting rooms?

7 Do they understand German?

Beispiel 2 Where is the photocopier?
Do you know where the photocopier is?

8 How many visitors are there?

9 Whose disc is this?

10 Where does he put the originals?

11 What's the name of their text programme?

12 How does this phone work?

13 When do they meet?

3 **Indirekte und direkte Fragen. Stellen Sie Fragen.** (→ SB3)

Beispiel Can you tell me where our visitors are?
Where are our visitors?

1 Do you know how much software is available for this computer?

____

2 Can you tell me what nationality she is?

____

3 Do you know if this photocopier uses special paper?

____

4 Can you tell me which button I press now?

____

5 Do you know how much jam they produce in one day?

____

6 Can you tell me where they sell their products?

____

4 **Relativpronomen. Ergänzen Sie die Hinweise mit 'who', 'which' oder 'where', bevor Sie das Kreuzworträtsel lösen!** (→ SB6)

1 a person who translates for two other people
2 the place _?_ a secretary works
3 things _?_ are not artificial
4 a place _?_ a company produces things
5 a person _?_ knows a lot about something
6 the day _?_ comes after Wednesday
7 a machine _?_ makes copies
8 a place _?_ people eat
9 a place _?_ you buy food
10 the country _?_ Fiat cars come from
11 a drink _?_ English and German people like

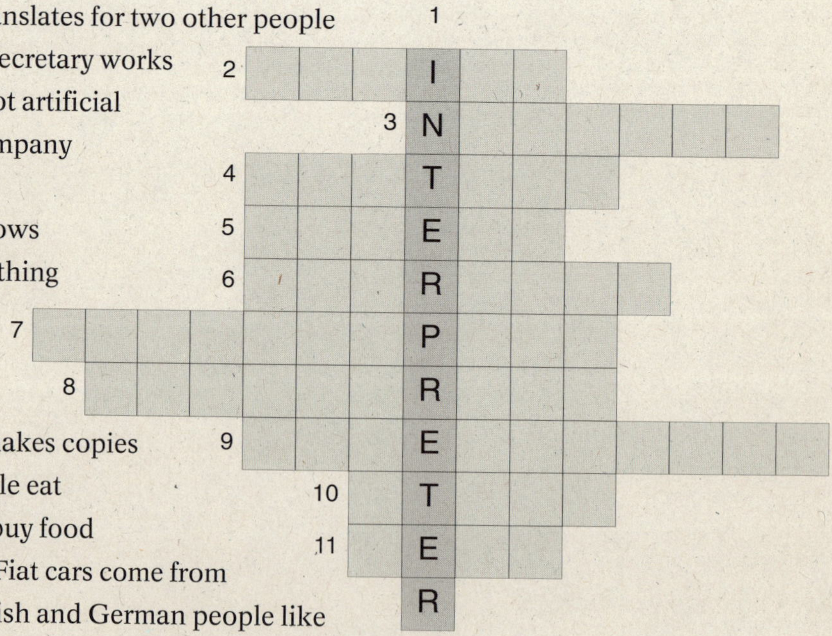

5 One/ones. Ergänzen Sie. (→ SB7)

1 Which office does he work in? - The big ______________ at the end.

2 Which room is it? - The third ______________ on the left.

3 Wait a moment, which details have you got there? - The ______________ from the new catalogue.

4 Can you give me the magazine? - Which ______________?

5 Where do I put these brochures? - The black-and-white ______________ go over here and the other ______________ go over there.

6 Relativpronomen. Ergänzen Sie mit 'who', 'which', 'where' oder 'with'. (→ SB7)

1 Turin is the city ______________ Fiat has its headquarters.

2 Which one is Robert McKay? - You know him. He's the one ______________ short black hair.

3 This is the equipment ______________ we need tomorrow.

4 That's the place ______________ they have got a new factory.

5 Which is the country ______________ paella comes from?

6 Mary Brown? Who's she? - She's the specialist ______________ comes in when we've got a problem.

7 This is the programme ______________ we use.

8 He is normally the one ______________ arrives first.

9 Which list do you need? - The one ______________ gives all the details.

10 Ms Davies is the person ______________ handles the administration.

7 Aussprache. Unterstreichen Sie den Teil des Wortes, der am meisten betont wird.

Beispiel presentation
presentation

1 international	2 normally	3 reception	4 receptionist
5 telephone	6 telephonist	7 administration	8 management
9 restaurant	10 director		

8 **Wortschatzwiederholung. Von jedem Wort oder Ausdruck geben Sie bitte das Gegenteil.**

1 a.m. <—->	p.m.	6 near <—->	________
2 ask <—->	________	7 a lot <—->	________
3 his <—->	________	8 artificial <—->	________
4 busy <—->	________	9 blond hair <—->	________
5 always <—->	________	10 downstairs <—->	________

9 **Allgemeine Wiederholung: Situationen. Ordnen Sie die Fragen und Antworten einander zu.**

1 Can you tell me where the canteen is?	7	Yes, that's right.
2 Do you know what time the meeting is?	____	Yes, a little.
3 Why don't I show you round?	____	It's at ten.
4 Is this seat taken?	____	Yes, of course I have.
5 Do you speak English?	____	It's on the ground floor.
6 Have you got a moment to check this?	____	No, it's free.
7 Is this Mr Roberts' office?	____	That's very kind.

Unit 6

1 **Verlaufsform der Gegenwart. Sehen Sie sich die Fluginformationen und Hotelreservierungen an, und ergänzen Sie den Text mit folgenden Verben: arrive, fly, leave, return, stay.** (→ SB2)

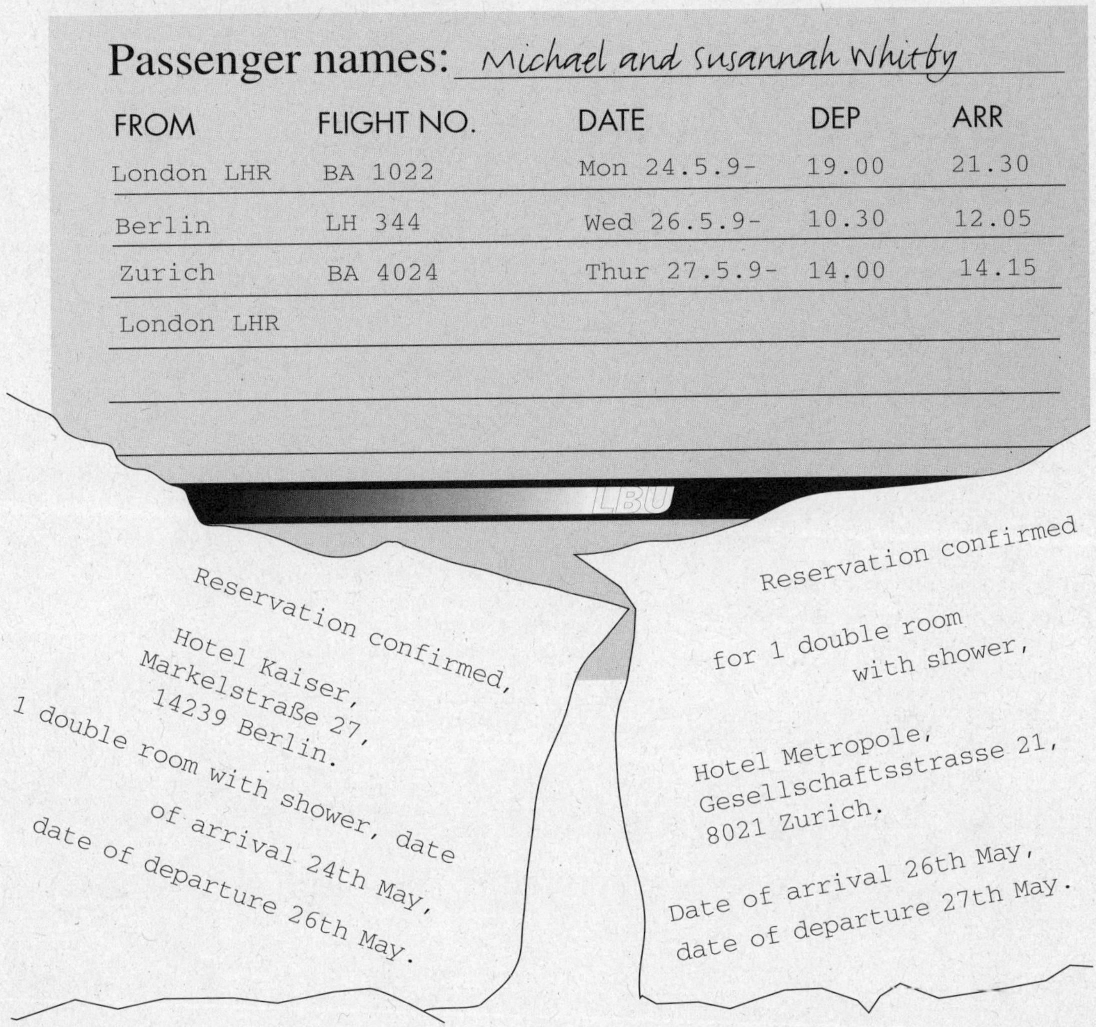

Passenger names: Michael and Susannah Whitby

FROM	FLIGHT NO.	DATE	DEP	ARR
London LHR	BA 1022	Mon 24.5.9-	19.00	21.30
Berlin	LH 344	Wed 26.5.9-	10.30	12.05
Zurich	BA 4024	Thur 27.5.9-	14.00	14.15
London LHR				

Reservation confirmed, Hotel Kaiser, Markelstraße 27, 14239 Berlin. 1 double room with shower, date of arrival 24th May, date of departure 26th May.

Reservation confirmed for 1 double room with shower, Hotel Metropole, Gesellschaftsstrasse 21, 8021 Zurich. Date of arrival 26th May, date of departure 27th May.

Michael and Susannah Whitby ________________ from London to Berlin on Monday next week. They ________________ London at 19.00. They ________________ in Berlin at 21.30. They ________________ two nights in Berlin at the Hotel Kaiser. At 10.30 on Wednesday morning they ________________ from Berlin to Zurich. They ________________ only one night in Zurich. They ________________ to London on the next day.

Unit 6

2 **Verlaufsform der Gegenwart, Datum und Uhrzeit. Michael Whitby fragt seine Frau nach den Einzelheiten ihrer Reise nächste Woche. Ergänzen Sie.** (→ SB2)

MW = Michael Whitby, SW = Susannah Whitby

MW When ______________________ (fly) from London?

SW ______________________ seven o'clock ______________________ the evening.

MW And what time ______________________ (arrive) in Berlin?

SW ______________________ half past nine.

MW How long ______________________ (stay) in Berlin?

SW Two nights.

MW Where ______________________ (go) after Berlin?

SW To Zurich, ______________________ Wednesday morning.

MW And where ______________________ (stay) __________ Wednesday night?

SW At the Hotel Metropole in Zurich.

MW When ______________________ (return) to London?

SW __________ two o'clock __________ the afternoon __________ the twenty-fifth.

3 **Verlaufsform der Gegenwart: Verneinung. Ergänzen Sie.** (→ SB2)

1 The Whitbys ______________________ (go) to Berlin on Sunday, they're going on Monday.

2 They ______________________ (return) to London from Berlin, but from Zurich.

3 Susannah ______________________ (fly) from London to Berlin with Lufthansa.

4 Susannah: "We ______________________ (stay) in Zurich two nights, but only one night."

5 Michael Whitby ______________________ (see) someone in Berlin, but Susannah is seeing someone.

6 The Whitbys ______________________ (travel) on Tuesday, but they are travelling on Monday, Wednesday and Thursday.

7 They ______________________ (fly) back to London with Swissair. They're returning with British Airways.

4 Want to/have to. Übersetzen Sie ins Deutsche. (→ SB9)

In our office we now have a flexitime system[1]. We don't have to work eight hours every day: we can choose[2] how many hours we want to work. The office opens at 7.30, but I don't have to go to work at 7.30 if I don't want to. We have to be in the office from 10.00 in the morning until 12.00, and then again from 2.00 until 4.00 in the afternoon. But at other times we can choose when we want to work. I can work six hours on one day and nine hours on the next if I want to.

[1] flexitime system = Gleitzeitsystem; [2] choose = wählen

____

____

____

____

____

____

____

____

5 Am Telefon. Wie würden Sie antworten? (→ SB10)

1 West's Garage, how can I help you?

- Oh, good morning, ____________________ Alan Taylor. I'm calling about …

2 I'm afraid she's not available at the moment.

- ____

3 Can I speak to Judith Black? (Sie ist im Büro)

- ____

4 Can I speak to Judith Black? (Sie ist im Büro, aber sehr beschäftigt).

- ____

5 Can I speak to Judith Black? (Sie spricht gerade mit einem Kunden, wird aber gleich wieder frei sein.)

- ____

Unit 6

6 Allgemeine Wiederholung: Fragen und Hilfsverben. Wie lautete die Frage?

1 No, I don't have to work tomorrow.

____

2 He normally leaves the office at about five past five.

____

3 She's coming back next Wednesday.

____

4 Yes, I speak some French, but not much.

____

5 I'm seeing her at four o'clock this afternoon.

____

6 Yes, they're coming with us.

____

7 No, we don't normally come to board meetings.

____

8 Yes, of course you can see the room.

____

7 Wiederholung: Präpositionen. Ergänzen Sie jeden Satz mit der richtigen Präposition (oder lassen Sie die Lücke leer, falls keine Präposition nötig ist).

1 She's arriving __________ the evening.

2 He has to travel __________ night.

3 The train leaves __________ three o'clock.

4 The meeting is __________ the fifth.

5 The presentation is __________ Friday.

6 Can you answer __________ the phone.

7 I am meeting him __________ the station.

8 I'll drive you __________ the hotel.

9 I want __________ see him now.

10 I can't __________ speak Spanish.

11 The factory is opening __________ January.

12 I'd like __________ come with you.

13 It's twenty __________ eight.

14 We are meeting __________ them tomorrow.

15 He works __________ BASF.

16 I'm going __________ Newcastle to see the exhibition.

17 Is Kim there? - Yes, but she's __________ the phone.

18 The printer is next __________ the computer.

19 The meeting rooms are __________ the second floor.

20 He has to change his flight because __________ the meeting.

8 Wortschatzwiederholung. Ergänzen Sie jeden Satz mit einem oder mehreren Wörtern.

1 When I want to book a flight I telephone the ____________________.

2 I'm flying to New York and back so I need a ____________________ ticket.

3 No, I'm not staying ____________________, I'm coming back the same day.

4 Make sure you call the airport and ____________________ the flight time before you leave.

5 I don't know where their office is, but they are sending someone to ____________________ me at the airport.

6 I have to fly early tomorrow. What time is the first ____________________ from Frankfurt?

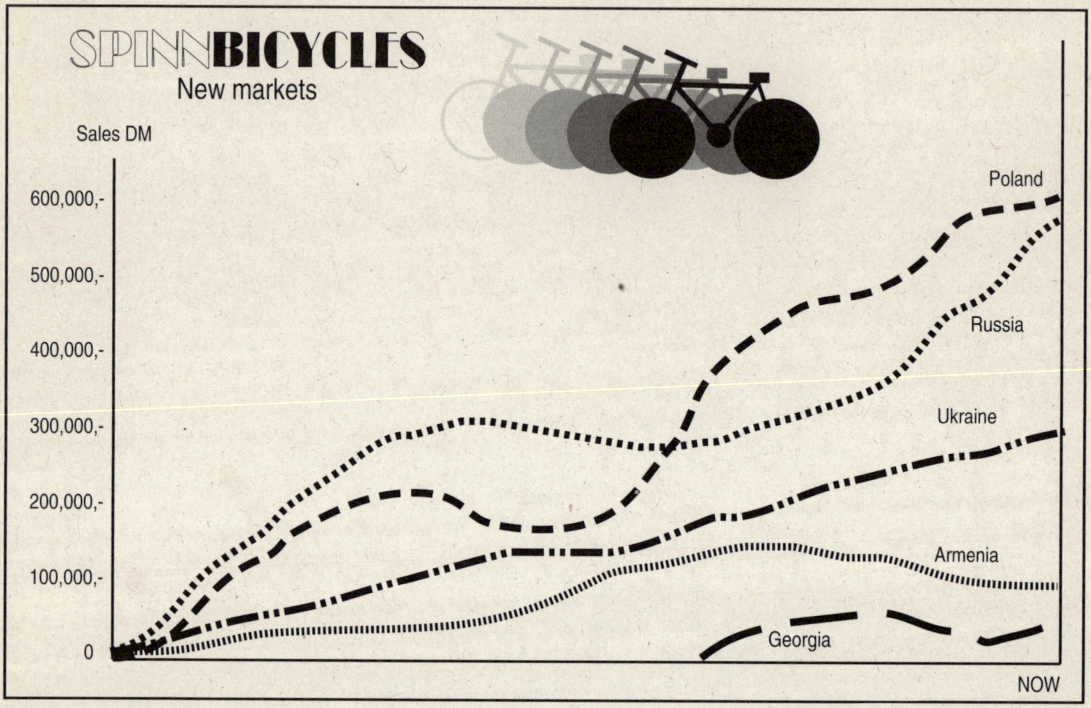

1 **Verlaufsform der Gegenwart. Ergänzen Sie mit: rise, fall, increase, decrease.** (→ SB2)

Sales of Spinn bicycles ______________________ nicely. Sales in Russia ____________ ____________ dramatically. They ______________________ fast in Poland, too. The market in Ukraine ______________________ quickly and steadily, but the Armenian market ______________________. The Georgian market ______________________ now.

2 **Adverbien der Art und Weise. Stimmen Sie zu.** (→ SB3)

Beispiel There is a dramatic rise in car sales.
- Yes, car sales are rising dramatically.

1 His English is perfect.

- ____

2 There is a slight rise in sales.

- ____

3 She is a very good worker.

- ____

4 There is a slow increase in our sales volume.

- ____

5 There is a steady fall in our number of foreign customers.

- ____

3 **Adjektiv oder Adverb? Unterstreichen Sie die richtige Form.** (→ SB2)

1 His English is perfectly / perfect.

2 This machine works quick / quickly.

3 Paul speaks German perfectly / perfect.

4 Anne speaks French very well / good.

5 Prices are rising very steadily / steady.

6 He's a slowly / slow worker.

7 Exports are decreasing dramatically / dramatic.

8 The increase in sales is dramatically / dramatic.

9 Which models are selling well / good this year?

10 Our new models are quickly / quick becoming bestsellers.

4 **Verlaufsform der Gegenwart.**
a) Ordnen Sie die Satzhälften einander zu. (→ SB3)

1 Sue is faxing	the new sales video.
2 Caroline is showing	the sales brochure from German into English.
3 Bob and James are working	the new building.
4 Richard is looking at	for the visitors.
5 Steven is translating	on the presentation.
6 The vistors are looking at	our visitors around the new building.
7 Tom is interpreting	→ a memo to our sales rep in Poland.
8 Mrs Campbell is waiting for	an important phone call.

b) Jetzt stellen Sie Fragen. (→ SB3)

Beispiel What is Sue doing?
She's faxing a memo to our sales rep in Poland.

1 ______________________________

She's showing our visitors around the new building.

2 ______________________________

They're looking at the new building.

3 ______________________________

She's waiting for an important phone call.

4 ______________________________

He's translating the sales brochure.

5 ______________________________

They're working on the presentation.

6 ______________________________

He's interpreting for the visitors.

7 ______________________________

He's looking at the new sales video.

c) Jetzt formulieren Sie Entschuldigungen bzw. Erklärungen. (→ SB4)

Beispiel Can Sue fax a letter to England now?
I'm afraid she can't. She's faxing a memo to our sales rep in Poland at the moment.

1 Can Caroline make this call?

____

____

2 Can Bob or James help me?

____

____

3 Can Richard look at this report?

4 Can Steve translate this letter?

5 Can the visitors meet the managing director now?

6 Can Tom interpret for us?

7 Can Mrs Campbell have a look at the sales video now?

5 **Verlaufsform der Gegenwart: Kurzantworten. Sehen Sie sich die Grafik in Übung 1 nochmal an und beantworten Sie die Fragen.** (→ SB7)

Beispiel Is the Georgian market rising?
Yes, it is.

1 Is the market in Russia rising?

2 Is the Ukrainian market decreasing?

3 Is the Polish market falling dramatically?

4 Is the Armenian market falling?

5 Is the Georgian market rising dramatically?

6 **Einfache Gegenwart: Kurzantworten. Beantworten Sie die Fragen über Tel-Fax AG.** (→ SB9)

Tel-Fax AG

HEADQUARTERS	Hannover
BRANCHES	2 (Hannover and Warsaw)
EMPLOYEES	32 in Hannover, 15 in Warsaw
DIRECTORS	Philip Adler, electrical engineer Place of work: Hannover Thomas Binz, communications expert Place of work: Warsaw
PLANS	- open a new branch in Prague - increase sales volume in Germany

Beispiel Does Tel-Fax AG have 3 branches?
No, it doesn't.

1 Does Philip Adler live in Hannover?

____

2 Does Thomas Binz work in Hannover, too?

____

3 Do the two directors work in Germany?

____

4 Does Tel-Fax have its headquarters in Hannover?

____

5 Does Tel-Fax have a branch in Prague?

____

6 Does the company have most of its employees in Poland?

____

7 Does it plan to increase its sales volume in Germany?

____

7 **Einfache und Verlaufsform der Gegenwart. Ergänzen Sie.** (→ SB10)

1 She usually _________________ (work) from 8.00 till 12,00, but this week she _________________ (work) in the afternoons.

2 _________________ (you/know) what time it is?

3 Who _________________ (use) the phone at the moment? I have to make an important call.

4 Alan _________________ (not speak) Spanish or German. He only _________________ (speak) French.

5 The childrens' models _________________ (not sell) very well this year.

6 Where _________________ (you/buy) the fruit usually?

7 Look! Jack _________________ (not work), he _________________ (read) a book!

8 I _________________ (not write) letters in English very often.

8 **Wortschatz. In diesem Rechteck sind 14 neue Wörter aus Unit 7 versteckt. Finden Sie sie?**

A	B	C	I	N	C	R	E	A	S	E	A	I	B	C	D
M	B	U	N	E	M	P	L	O	Y	M	E	N	T	P	C
E	F	A	V	F	F	E	X	P	A	E	X	T	A	F	O
N	A	F	E	C	N	W	W	T	K	M	C	E	X	H	S
T	L	E	S	X	I	J	H	T	K	O	H	R	E	N	T
R	L	A	T	A	L	T	X	T	A	L	A	E	S	P	N
E	O	P	M	G	D	U	M	M	A	R	N	S	Q	E	R
S	T	Q	E	E	T	I	N	G	U	V	G	T	W	R	X
Y	Z	A	N	R	I	S	E	R	B	C	E	R	D	C	E
F	G	S	T	A	T	E	M	E	N	T	E	A	H	E	I
J	K	L	S	T	E	A	D	I	L	Y	Y	T	O	N	P
S	H	D	R	E	D	Z	Q	R	S	T	K	E	U	T	V
W	S	L	O	W	L	Y	X	Y	Z	A	B	S	C	D	E

Unit 8

1 **Steigerung des Adjektivs. Vergleichen Sie die Familien Zimmerli und Stanton.**
(→ SB3)

Rudi Zimmerli and Jane Stanton are computer engineers.
Rudi is 25 years old. He works for a small electronics firm in Zurich, Switzerland. He and his wife (Frau), Isabelle, work full-time (ganztags). They have a 3-room flat (Wohnung) in a small town outside Zurich.

Jane Stanton is 32 years old. She works for a big British electronics firm in Aberdeen, Scotland. Her husband (Ehemann), Joseph, is a teacher, but he hasn't got a full-time job at the moment. They live in a small house (Haus) - 6 rooms - 5 km from Aberdeen.

	Rudi & Isabelle:	Jane & Joseph:
Total salary per month (in £)	3,040	1,200
	Rudi:	Jane:
Holidays per year	20	20
Working week	42	40
Working day	7.30 - 5.30 not including lunch	9 - 5 including lunch
Lunchtime	2 hours	1 hour
Rent per month	652	290

1 The Zimmerlis' rent is ______________________ the Stantons' rent.

2 The Zimmerlis have got ______________ rooms ______________ the Stantons.

3 Rudi has got as ______________ holidays ______________ Jane.

4 Jane can leave the office at five. That's 30 minutes ______________________

______________________ Rudi.

5 Jane's lunch time is ____________________ Rudi's.

6 Rudi's working week is two hours ____________________ Jane's.

7 Jane works __________ hours per day ____________________ Rudi.

8 The Stantons' total salary is much ____________________ than the Zimmerlis'.

2 **Schottland und die Schweiz. Ergänzen Sie mit der Steigerungsform von: low, high, long, short, early.** (→ SB4)

1 Rents in Switzerland are normally ____________________ in Scotland.

2 A working day in Scotland is normally not ____________________ a working day in Switzerland.

3 Lunchtimes in Scotland are normally ____________________ in Switzerland.

4 Salaries in Scotland are normally ____________________ in Switzerland.

5 A working day in Switzerland is normally ____________________ in Scotland.

6 Rents in Scotland are normally not ____________________ rents in Switzerland.

7 Holidays in Switzerland are normally ____________________ holidays in Scotland.

3 **Steigerung des Adjektivs. Formulieren Sie jeweils zwei Widersprüche wie im Beispiel.** (→ SB5)

Beispiel Salaries for engineers are normally higher than for bankers.
No, salaries for bankers are normally as high as for engineers.
No, salaries for bankers are normally higher than for engineers.

1 Working hours for salespeople are longer than working hours for teachers.

____

____

2 A modern flat in Munich is more expensive than a modern flat in Zurich.

____

____

3 Salaries in Frankfurt are normally higher than in Paris.

____

____

4 A job in a city is more interesting than a job in a small town.

____

____

4 **Steigerung des Adjektivs. Ergänzen Sie die Tabelle.** (→ SB6)

1	small	smaller	smallest	↔ big	bigger	biggest
2	short	________	________	________	________	________
3	easy	________	________	________	________	________
					________	________
4	old	________	________	________	________	________
5	good	________	________	________	________	________
6	low	________	________	________	________	________
7	expensive	________	________	________	________	________
		________	________			

5 **2. Steigerungsstufe. Vervollständigen Sie mit der 2.Steigerungsstufe von: short, big, old, long, good, small, early.** (→ SB6)

1 ________________ official working week in Europe is in Switzerland.

2 One of the ________________ working days is in Spain.

3 German workers have ________________ holiday deal: 30 working days.

4 Germans have ________________ holidays.

5 Our company has got five branches. ________________ branch, with 350 employees, is in Munich, and ________________ branch, with only 42 employees, is in Ravensburg.

6 I've got a meeting in Rome tomorrow morning. What time is ________________ flight?

7 There are three versions of this software: a 1987 version, a 1993 version, and this version. The 1987 version is ________________ one.

6 **Steigerung von Adjektiven. Lesen Sie die drei Stellenanzeigen und die Notizen, die ein junger Programmierer sich dazu gemacht hat, und ergänzen Sie die unten stehenden Sätze.** (→ SB7)

Computer programmer,
ATZ Ltd. Work in the centre of Cambridge for a small but good company, be part of a great team. Starting salary £17,000.

Send CV: Ms Jane Tanning, ATZ Ltd, Market Hill, Cambridge, tel 0223-3046677.

Working hours:
8 am - 4pm,
45 minutes lunch break
40 minutes travel time from home
Holidays per year 18 days (first year), 35 employees.

COMPUTER PROGRAMMER
-
TECHTIP.
American company in Cambridge is looking for a top programmer for our CAD division.
Salary £14,000.

Contact Mr M Manning, 0223-265753.

1,300 employees,
travel time 15 minutes
Working hours 8-4 or 9-5,
1 hour lunch, lunchtime flexible
20 holidays per year,
one week of holiday must be at Christmas.

Computer programmer:
Balmar & Brothers Ltd.
Salary £9,000 plus free (new, modern) 4-room flat 1 minute from office. If you have experience, energy, and like teamwork, contact us at 0223-474351.

16 employees,
no travel time
Low salary but no rent for flat
Holidays fixed:
14 days in July,
14 days in January.
Working hours very flexible:
35 hours per week when I want!

1 The salary at Techtip is ________________ the salary at ATZ, but the job at Balmar offers ______________ salary of all three.

2 The travel time for the job at ATZ is ______________.

3 The travel time for the job at Techtip is ______________________ for the job at ATZ, but the travel time for the job at Balmer is the ______________ - zero!

4 ATZ offers ______________ salary but ______________ holidays per year.

5 The holidays at Balmar are ________________ flexible.

6 The working hours at ATZ are ________________ flexible than at Techtip, but the holidays at ATZ are ________________ flexible.

7 Techtip has ________________ employees than ATZ, but Balmar has ________________.

7 Wiederholung: Zahlen. Welche Firma und was ist gemeint?

1 thirteen hundred

Techtip The number of __________________________

2 seventeen thousand

____________________________________ The ____________________________________

3 oh two two three, four seven four three five one

____________________________________ The ____________________________________

4 three quarters of an hour

____________________________________ The ____________________________________

5 twenty-eight

____________________________________ The number of __________________________

6 thirty-six and a quarter

____________________________________ The ____________________________________

8 Wiederholung: Kurzantworten. Beantworten Sie.

1 Are ATZ offering the best salary? Yes, they are.

2 Does Techtip's advertisement say there is a flat with the job? ________________________

3 Do Techtip have the most employees? ____________________________________

4 Is there an hour's lunch break at ATZ? ____________________________________

5 Are all three companies looking for a programmer? ____________________________________

6 Does the person who is looking for the job live far from Techtip? ____________________

9 **Wortschatz. Ergänzen Sie.**

1 Austria Austrian	5 England ____________
2 France ____________	6 Holland ____________
3 Germany ____________	7 Spain ____________
4 Britain ____________	8 Europe ____________

Telebelle GmbH: a true European company!

The managing director of Telebelle is (GB) ____________. She is English, from Bath. The assistant director is (F) ____________. Two of the three secretaries are (NL) ____________, one is from (CH) ____________. The head engineer is (D) ____________ and his assistant is from Switzerland. The assistant speaks (F) ____________, (D) ____________, (E) ____________ and English. We are a very (EC) ____________ company, so of course we have a coffee machine from (I) ____________!

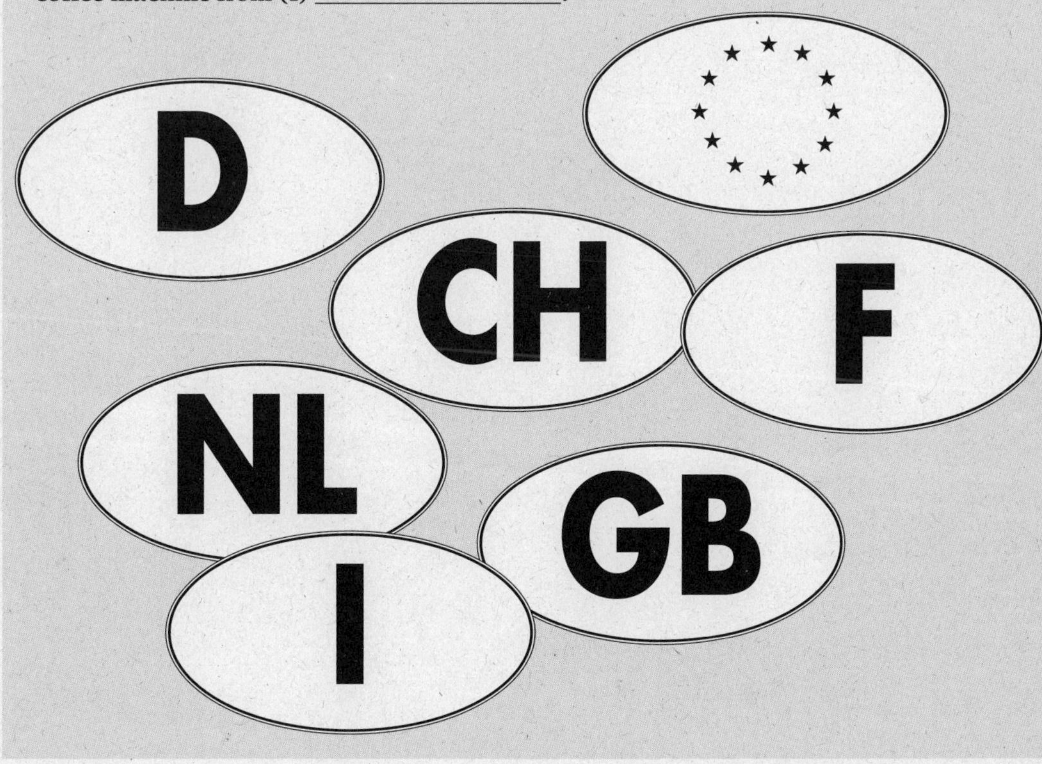

Test 2

Kreuzen Sie in diesem Test die jeweils richtige Lösung an. Für jede Aufgabe gibt es nur eine richtige Lösung.

Die Firma 'LeTouche', mit Filialen europaweit, hat für junge Manager ihres Unternehmens eine Woche Management-Training organisiert. Das Seminar findet in London statt und die Teilnehmer/innen kommen von den verschiedenen Filialen dorthin.

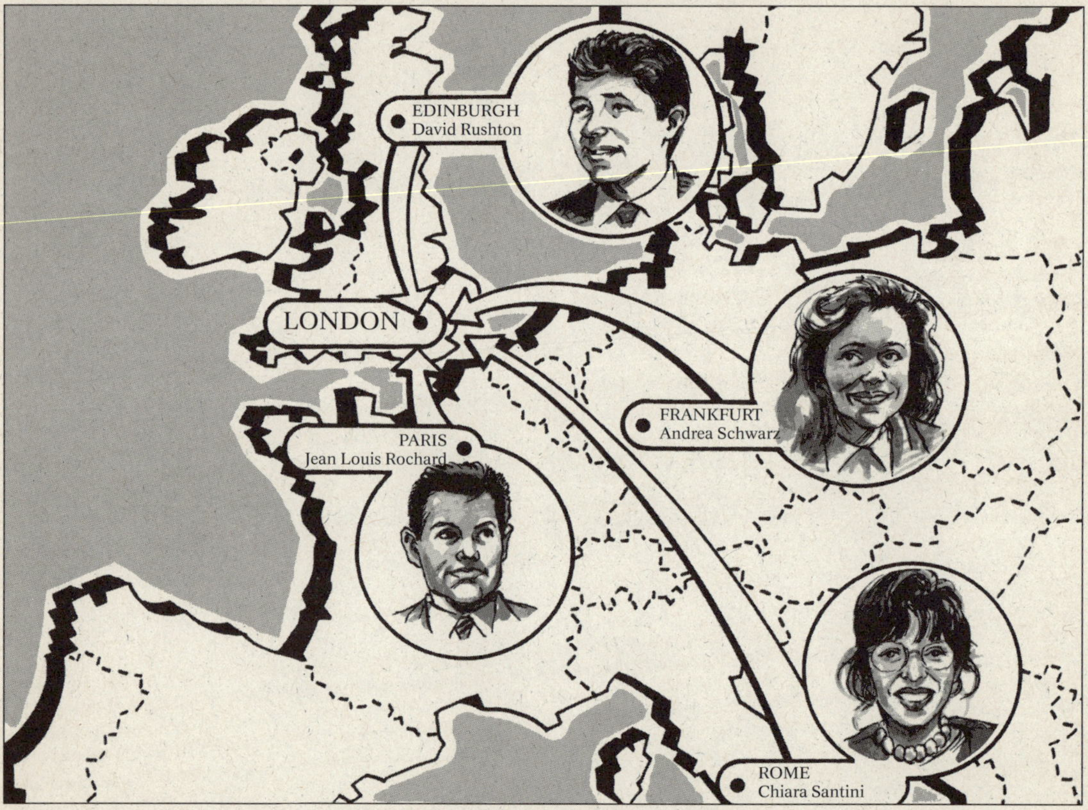

1 Wortschatz

David Rushton möchte seinen Flug nach London buchen.

1 I'd like to book a ... to London, please.
- a flight ❏
- b fly ❏
- c plane ❏
- d travel ❏

2 Certainly, sir. Which day would you like to ... ?
- a drive ❏
- b flight ❏
- c travel ❏
- d trip ❏

3 ... the early evening.
- a At Thursday at ❏
- b At Thursday on ❏
- c On Thursday at ❏
- d On Thursday in ❏

4 Is that a single or ... ticket?
- a back ❏
- b double ❏
- c return ❏
- d there and back ❏

5 I will call you back tomorrow and ... .
- a check in ❏
- b confirm ❏
- c inform ❏
- d put you through ❏

2 Situationen

1 Der Kursleiter, Alan Miller, führt die Teilnehmergruppe kurz in der Zentrale herum. Er sagt: 'OK, why don't I ... first'.

- a look you around ❏
- b see you around ❏
- c show you around ❏
- d show you where ❏

2 The canteen is ... floor.

- a in the first ❏
- b in the second ❏
- c on the first ❏
- d to the second ❏

3 Im Konferenzraum tut sich jemand schwer mit dem Videogerät. Sie bieten Hilfe an. Er sagt: '...'.

- a It's very nice. ❏
- b That's right. ❏
- c That's very kind. ❏
- d You're very friendly. ❏

4 Die Konferenz hat gerade begonnen, als das Telefon klingelt. Sie gehen dran. Jemand will Mr Miller sprechen, aber er kann gerade nicht. Sie sagen: '...'.

- a Can I leave a message? ❏
- b I'll put you through. ❏
- c I'm afraid his line is busy at the moment. ❏
- d I'm afraid Mr Miller's not available at the moment. ❏

3 Grammatik

Der Kursleiter gibt den Teilnehmern jetzt einen kurzen Überblick über die Tätigkeit der Firma in Europa.

1 The volume of work ... near the end of the financial year.

- a always increases ❏
- b always is increasing ❏
- c does always increase ❏
- d is always increasing ❏

2 As you can see, at the moment our turnover (= Umsatz) in France and Germany ... .

- a are rising ❏
- b does rise ❏
- c is rising ❏
- d rises ❏

3 We haven't got this year's figures for Italy yet. Our Rome branch ... on them now.

- a are working ❏
- b is working ❏
- c work ❏
- d works ❏

Jetzt ist Kaffeepause und die Teilnehmer reden über die verschiedenen Filialen, wo sie arbeiten.

4 Am I right that salaries in the UK are ... in Germany?

- a fewer as ❏
- b fewer than ❏
- c lower as ❏
- d lower than ❏

5 We don't get ... weeks holiday in Italy as in Germany.

- a a lot ❏
- b as long ❏
- c as many ❏
- d as much ❏

6 Tell me, which of those two women is the trainer from New York? - ... is writing on the flipchart.

- a The tall one which ❏
- b The tall one who ❏
- c The tall which ❏
- d The tall who ❏

Unit 9

1 **Über die Zukunft mit 'will' reden. Machen Sie Prognosen für das vierte Quartal.** (→ SB1)

Beispiel sales in Germany
They think sales in Germany will rise by DM 20,000.

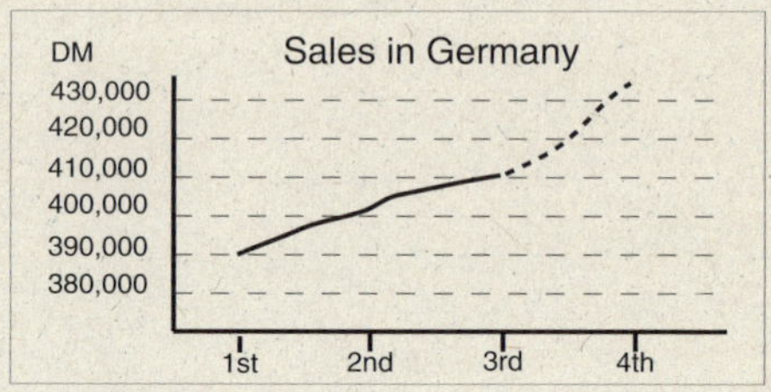

1

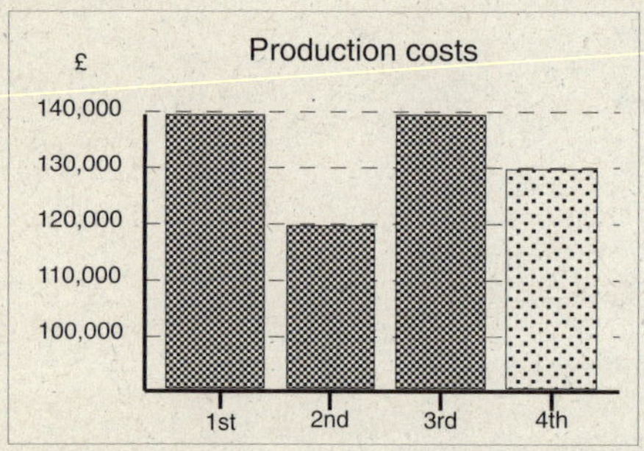

2

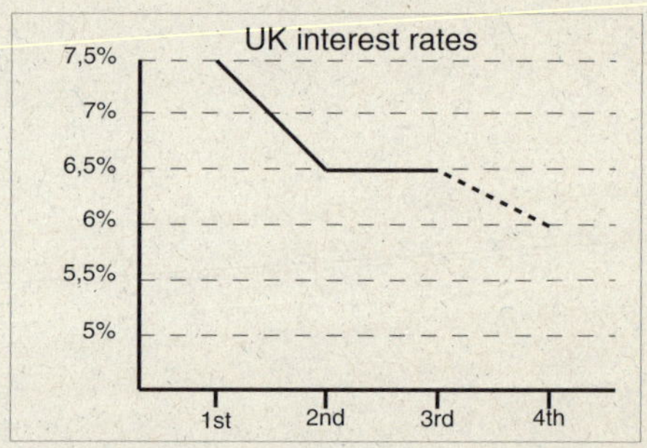

3

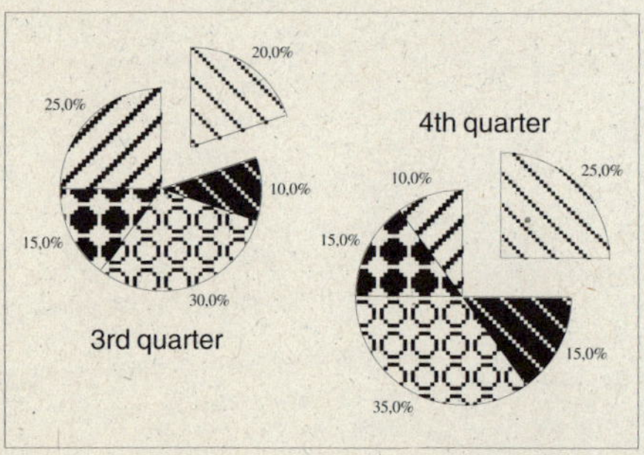

4

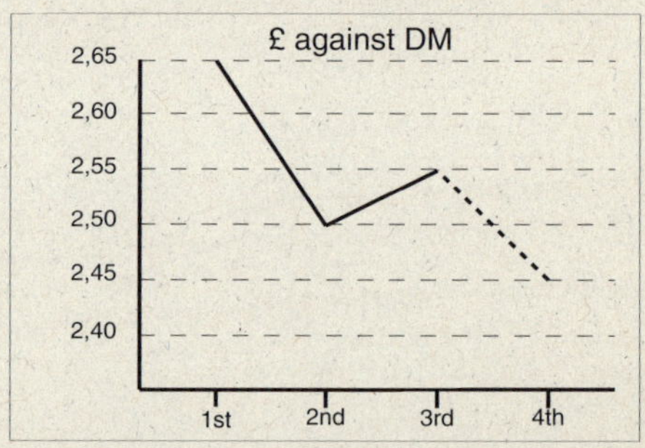

1 production costs

____

2 UK interest rates

____

3 market share[1]

____

4 the pound against[2] the Deutschmark

____

[1]market share = Marktanteil; [2]against = gegenüber

2 **will/won't. Sehen Sie sich die Grafiken nochmal an und bilden Sie Fragen und Antworten.** (→ SB2)

Beispiel sales/fall
Will sales fall? - No, sales won't fall. They'll rise.

1 production costs/rise

2 interest rates/go up

3 market share/decrease

4 pound/rise against the Deutschmark

3 **will/won't. Stellen Sie Fragen und beantworten Sie sie mit 'No'.** (→ SB2)

Beispiel she/leave the company - stay
Will she leave the company, do you think?
No, she won't. I think she'll stay.

1 he/be in the office tomorrow - in London

2 she/be available for a meeting - away

3 the new model/be more expensive - cheaper

4 they/get a table at this time of day - restaurant full

____

____

5 they/have the meeting in Germany - England

____

____

4 **Angebote und Bitten. Bringen Sie folgende Dialogteile in die richtige Reihenfolge, indem Sie 1, 2, 3 usw in die Kästchen schreiben.** (→ SB4)

- [ ] Good morning, my name's Claire Hawthorne. I'm here to give a computer training course to your accounts department. Could you tell me which room we are using?
- [ ] There's a car park next to the building. Shall I show you where it is?
- [ ] Where shall I leave it then?
- [ ] Thank you. Before we look at the room, could someone perhaps help me to bring one or two things in from the car?
- [1] Good morning, can I help you?
- [ ] Of course. Is it at the front of the building?
- [ ] No, it's OK for five or ten minutes to unload, but you'll get a parking ticket[1] if you leave it there for longer.
- [ ] Yes. Will it be OK to leave it there?
- [ ] Oh yes, thank you very much.
- [ ] Oh yes, of course. I'll show you the room - it's not very easy to find.

[1]parking ticket = Strafzettel

5 **Verben mit 'ing'. Bilden Sie Fragen und sagen Sie dann, was Sie persönlich vorziehen.** (→ SB7)

Beispiel eat in the canteen/eat in a restaurant
Which do you prefer, eating in the canteen or eating in a restaurant?
- I prefer eating in a restaurant.

1 drive to the office/take the bus

____

____

2 use a blackboard/use a flipchart

3 speak English on the phone/speak German

4 work in your office/work at home[1]

5 fly/take the train

6 learn English/go out for a drink?

[1]at home = zu Hause

6 **Verben mit 'ing'. Ergänzen Sie. Verwenden Sie jedes Verb nur einmal.** (→ SB7)

drink	eat in	fly in	learn	pay	sit in	~~travel~~	visit	work

Beispiel I like trains.
I like travelling in trains.

1 I dislike long meetings.

2 I hate computers.

3 I love planes.

4 I dislike fast-food restaurants.

5 I like foreign cities.

____

6 I like beer.

____

7 I hate taxes.

____

8 I love English.

____

7 **Sätze mit 'if'. Sehen Sie sich die Grafiken in Übung 1 nochmal an und bilden Sie Sätze.** (→ SB9)

Beispiel If sales rise by £20,000, they'll be £430,000.

1 production costs fall/£10,000

____

2 interest rates fall/half a per cent

____

3 our market share increase/5%

____

4 pound go down against the mark/10 pfennigs

____

____

8 **Allgemeine Wiederholung: Verben mit 'to', ohne 'to' oder als 'ing'-Form. Ergänzen Sie. Verwenden Sie jedes Verb nur einmal.**

be	finish	go	know	read	show	speak	visit	~~work~~

Beispiel I hate ..... late in the evening.
I hate working late in the evening.

1 I like ______________ out to restaurants.

2 Can you ______________ French?

3 Will there ______________ any tables free?

4 I would like ______________________ the report before the meeting.

5 I have ______________________ the report before Friday.

6 I like ______________________ other cities.

7 Would you please ______________________ me where you keep the files?

8 Does he ______________________ how to use this programme?

9 **Wortschatzwiederholung. In diesem Quadrat sind 20 Wörter versteckt, die mit Essen und Trinken zu tun haben. Finden Sie sie?**

~~L~~	~~U~~	~~N~~	~~C~~	~~H~~	D	A	J	W	I	N	E
I	E	T	E	A	I	O	E	A	T	D	I
N	C	P	W	N	N	H	S	F	M	R	M
G	A	R	A	C	N	C	A	O	B	I	E
R	N	B	I	G	E	O	L	O	I	N	N
E	T	I	T	V	R	F	T	D	U	K	U
D	E	L	E	Q	W	F	F	R	U	I	T
I	E	L	R	X	T	E	K	B	E	E	R
E	N	J	A	M	D	E	S	U	G	A	R
N	F	S	M	A	R	M	A	L	A	D	E
T	R	E	S	T	A	U	R	A	N	T	Y

Unit 10

1 **Was/were. Ergänzen Sie die Fragen und beantworten Sie sie.** (→ SB2)

Alison and Jim

Ian

Beispiel ... Ian on holiday last week?
Was Ian on holiday last week?
- No, he wasn't.

1 ____________________ Alison and Jim on holiday in Spain last week?

- ____.

2 ____________________ Ian in the office last week?

- ____.

3 ____________________ Alison and Jim in the office last week?

- ____.

4 ____________________ the weather[1] good in Spain?

- ____.

5 ____________________ the weather good in England?

- ____.

[1]weather = Wetter

2 **Fragen und Kurzantworten mit 'did/didn't'. Stellen Sie Fragen und beantworten Sie sie.** (→ SB3)

Beispiel Jim/arrange any meetings/No
Did Jim arrange any meetings last week?
- No, he didn't.

1 Ian/start work early/Yes

____

2 Alison/call any customers/No

____

3 Alison and Jim/play tennis/Yes

____

4 Ian/play tennis/No

____

5 Jim and Alison/work hard/No

____

6 Ian/work hard/Yes

____

3 **Vergangenheitsform. Ergänzen Sie.** (→ SB 5)

Beispiel She ... them last week. (call)
She called them last week.

1 He __________________ the meeting last month. (arrange)

2 They __________________ the meeting last week. (miss)

3 She __________________ the sales figures yesterday. (fax)

4 We __________________ him a room in the Metropole Hotel last time. (book)

5 He __________________ busy yesterday afternoon. (be)

6 They __________________ work early last Friday. (finish)

7 I __________________ the figures carefully before the meeting. (check)

8 She __________________ work early this morning. (start)

9 I __________________ them to the Rose and Crown restaurant last time. (invite)

4 **Auf Vorschläge und Fragen reagieren. Wie würden Sie in den folgenden Situationen antworten?** (→ SB6)

1 Is Thursday convenient? (Sagen Sie, daß es das leider nicht ist. Sagen Sie, daß Sie den ganzen Tag in London sein müssen.)

____

2 Is 2.00 all right? (Sagen Sie, daß 15.00 Uhr günstiger für Sie wäre.)

____

3 When will you be able to give me a date? (Sagen Sie, daß Sie ihm morgen Bescheid geben.)

____

4 Are you able to come to the meeting this afternoon? (Sagen Sie, daß Sie eigentlich die Sitzung ändern möchten. Fragen Sie, ob Sie sich morgen treffen könnten.)

____

____

5 How about next week? (Für Sie ist das prima.)

____

5 **Vergangenheitsform unregelmäßiger Verben. Ergänzen Sie.** (→ SB 8)

Beispiel Last week I ... him a long letter. (write)
Last week I wrote him a long letter.

1 We ____________ a letter from them last week. (get)

2 I ____________ the disc back in the box after I used it. (put)

3 The last meeting ____________ at 8.00 in the morning. (begin)

4 I ____________ home early last night. (go)

5 He ____________ that there was a later train. (say)

6 They ____________ French at the meeting so I wasn't able to understand. (speak)

7 I ____________ £50 in the street yesterday. (find)

8 Annette Barker? Yes, she's here somewhere. I ____________ her when I came in. (see)

9 I ____________ the managing director when I was there. (meet)

6 **Gemischte Vergangenheitsformen. Ergänzen Sie die Sätze. (?) bedeutet, daß Sie eine Frage, (✔), daß Sie eine bejahte Aussage, (✘), daß Sie eine verneinte Aussage bilden sollen.** (→ SB 8)

Beispiel ... her this morning? (you, see)(?)
Did you see her this morning?

1 ______________________________ their prices last month. (they, increase) (✔)

2 ______________________________ very well last year. (that model, sell) (✘)

3 ______________________________ the figures before you faxed them? (you, check) (?)

4 I'm afraid ______________________________ time to call you this morning. (I, have) (✘)

5 ______________________________ to him this morning. (I, speak) (✔)

6 ______________________________ the time of the meeting. (he, know) (✘)

7 What time ______________________________ this morning? (they, arrive) (?)

8 ______________________________ the letter back in the file. (he, put) (✘)

9 ______________________________ you the time of the flight? (she, tell) (?)

7 **Allgemeine Wiederholung: Gemischte Zeitformen. Ergänzen Sie die Sätze mit nur einem Wort pro Lücke.**

1 Do you think office rents ______________ rise much next year?
- No, I'm sure they ______________.

2 What ______________ the exchange rate for the pound today?
- I'm afraid I ______________ know. I ______________ look in the newpaper this morning.

3 ______________ you tell him about the new plan when you ______________ him yesterday?

4 I ______________ know whether the food in the canteen is good or bad. I never ______________ there.

5 ______________ they increase the tax on alcohol next April?
- Yes, I'm sure that they ______________ increase it. They ______________ it every year. Last year they ______________ it by 5%.

6 ______________ that model selling well at the moment?

- Yes, it ______________ selling very well. Last month we ______________ over 3000 units and I think we ______________ sell over 4000 by the end of this month.

7 Are you ______________ to the office party next week?

- Oh yes, I ______________ to the office party every year.

8 Wortschatzwiederholung. In diesem Quadrat sind 16 Wörter versteckt, die mit Reisen und Verkehr zu tun haben. Finden Sie sie?

~~V~~	~~I~~	~~S~~	~~I~~	~~T~~	C	D	L	A	T	E	F
G	A	G	E	D	A	R	T	F	O	A	L
D	L	E	A	V	E	I	R	D	B	I	Y
O	A	B	K	M	J	V	I	C	A	R	C
V	R	O	F	V	H	E	P	R	N	E	A
E	R	A	B	R	O	A	D	O	W	L	I
R	I	N	P	U	Y	Q	T	R	I	P	R
N	V	B	O	O	K	E	X	M	H	O	L
I	E	T	K	F	L	I	G	H	T	I	I
G	T	I	C	K	E	T	A	L	T	P	N
H	S	E	F	C	O	N	F	I	R	M	E
T	S	R	J	E	Q	Z	P	L	A	N	E

1 **Das Perfekt. Sarah Roberts ist für die Lagerkontrolle in einer großen Plattenfirma zuständig. Stellen Sie und beantworten Sie Fragen.** (→ SB2)

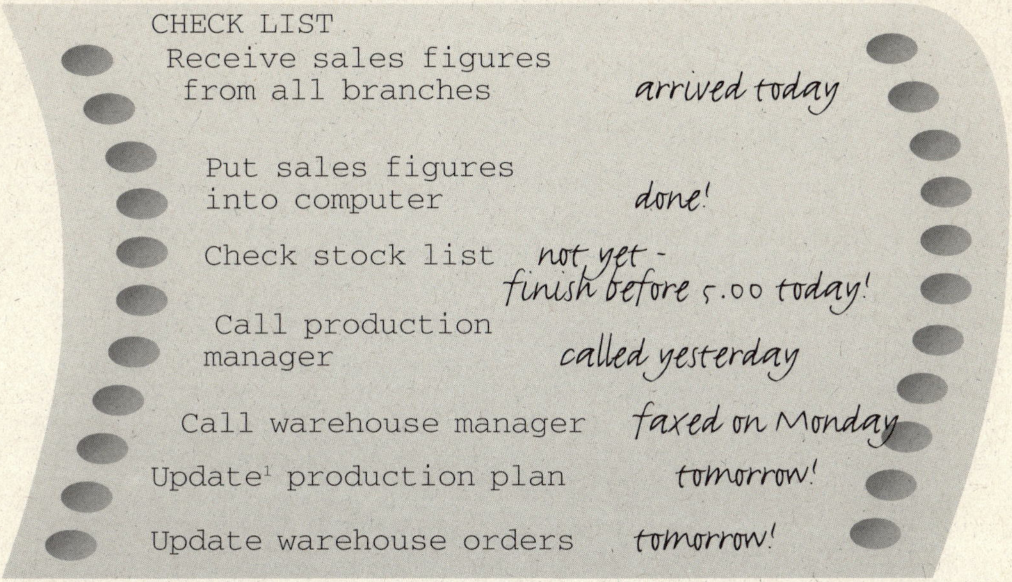

[1]update = aktualisieren

Beispiel receive sales figures from all branches/this month
Has she received the sales figures from all the branches this month?
- Yes, she has.

1 put sales figures into computer/this week

___

___

2 check stock list/today

___

___

3 phone production manager/this week

___

___

4 update production plan/today

___

___

5 fax warehouse manager/this week

____

____

6 update orders from warehouse/this week

____

____

2 **Das Perfekt. Ergänzen Sie.** (→ SB3)

1 (it/not be) __________________ possible to speak to him this week.

2 (you/speak) __________________ to the employees about the new system?

3 (he/not take) __________________ the catalogue with him.

4 (they/not eat) __________________ lunch yet.

5 (he/go) __________________ home.

6 (we/give) __________________ them 5.5% bulk discount.

7 (you/find) __________________ the engineer yet?

8 (I/write) __________________ to him several times but he hasn't replied.

3 **Vergangenheit oder Perfekt? Bilden Sie Sätze.** (→ SB6)

Beispiel he/just bring/the contract
He has just brought the contract.

1 she sell/her car/two days ago

____

2 they reply/to our letter/yet?

____

3 he/never use/this programme/before

____

4 I buy/a new computer/last week - how much/it cost?

____

____

5 they/just buy/a fax machine

6 I/already see/their factory

7 you/ever visit/their headquarters?

8 he find/a new job/for next year

9 they change/their phone number/last month

4 **Perfekt oder Vergangenheit? Wie lautete die Frage?** (→ SB 6)

Beispiel Tell him? Of course I did.
Did you tell him?

1 When? Yesterday. And I'm seeing him tomorrow too.

2 Call him back? Yes, I did, immediately.

3 No, I haven't called him this week, but I did last week.

4 How often? I think I've been there three times.

5 To France? No, I haven't, not recently.

6 The report? Yes, she's already finished it.

7 Your order? Yes, we despatched it last Friday.

8 Malt whisky? No, never.

5 **Allgemeine Wiederholung: gemischte Zeitformen. Sehen Sie sich die Checkliste in Übung 1 nochmal an und ergänzen Sie den Text.**

Sarah Roberts: I am responsible for stock control so I_______________ (receive) the sales figures and stock details every week from all our branches. They all _______________ (arrive) earlier this morning and I immediately _______________ (put) them in the computer. The computer normally _______________ (take) about ten minutes to coordinate the figures and to identify possible problems. I _______________ (not check) the computer data yet but I _______________ (do) this before I _______________ (go) home today. Each week I _______________ (contact) the production manager and the warehouse manager to inform them of changes in quantities and priorities.
I _______________ (contact) both of them already this week. I called the production manager yesterday and _______________ (fax) the warehouse manager on Monday. Every month we _______________ (update) the production plan. We _______________ (not update) it yet this month. I _______________ (update) it tomorrow.

6 **Bestellung und Lieferung. Übersetzen Sie diese Sätze ins Englische.**

1 Wie war die Bestellnummer?

____

2 Welche Menge möchten Sie?

____

3 Bekommen wir einen Mengenrabatt?

____

4 Ich werde die Bestätigung durchfaxen.

____

5 Ich rufe wegen unserer Bestellung an.

____

6 Leider können wir erst nächsten Monat liefern.

____

7 Wir werden es heute abschicken.

8 Vielleicht gibt es ein Problem bei der Reederei.

9 Die Lieferung hätte letzte Woche ankommen sollen.

7 **Allgemeine Wiederholung: Situationen. Wie würden Sie antworten?**

1 How do you do?

2 Can you show me how this works?

3 Thank you very much.

4 Excuse me, where's the canteen?

5 I'm afraid her line is busy at the moment.

6 Would you like to come to dinner?

7 Is the 23rd convenient for you?

8 Excuse me, do you speak English?

Test 3

Kreuzen Sie in diesem Test die jeweils richtige Lösung an. Für jede Aufgabe gibt es nur eine richtige Lösung.

Sean O'Brien, Ausbildungsassistent einer Firma in Manchester, England, hat einen Management-Training-Kurs für Mittelmanager/innen organisiert. Er hat alles sorgfätig geplant.

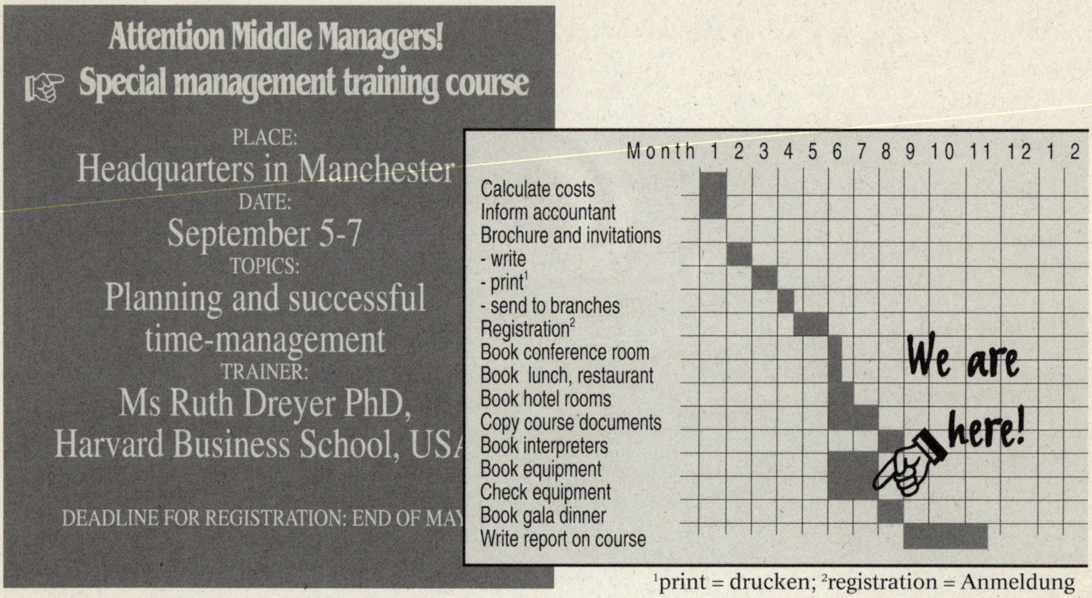

[1]print = drucken; [2]registration = Anmeldung

1 Grammatik

Es ist jetzt Mitte Juli.

1 Mr O'Brien ... invitations in April. ❑
- a has sent ❑
- b sending ❑
- c sent ❑
- d will send ❑

2 Mr O'Brien ... the report on the course yet.
- a hasn't written ❑
- b has written ❑
- c will write ❑
- d writes ❑

3 Mr O'Brien ... the gala dinner in August.
- a has booked ❑
- b will book ❑
- c will eat ❑
- d won't book ❑

4 Mr O'Brien ... the conference room and the hotel rooms already.
- a books ❑
- b has booked ❑
- c is booking ❑
- d will book ❑

5 Mr O'Brien ... the registrations by the end of May.
- a gets ❑
- b got ❑
- c has got ❑
- d will get ❑

6 If there are no foreigners at the course, Mr O'Brien ... book interpreters.
- a didn't ❑
- b doesn't ❑
- c isn't ❑
- d won't ❑

2 Situationen

Ein Kursteilnehmer aus Düsseldorf, Albert Müller (AM), telefoniert mit Herrn O'Brien (O'B) und stellt ein paar Fragen.

AM Hello, Mr O'Brien. This is Mr Müller from Düsseldorf. I'm staying in Manchester on business after the course. ...(1)... book a room for me from the 5th to the 10th?

O'B Of course. ...(2)... the same hotel as last time?

AM That would be very nice. Thank you.

O'B I'll call back this afternoon to confirm. Is that convenient?

AM ...(3)... . I'll be in a meeting.

O'B Shall I call tomorrow then?

AM ...(4)...

1 a Can I ❑
b Could you ❑
c Shall I ❑
d Would you like ❑

2 a Could you book ❑
b Let me book ❑
c Shall I book ❑
d Would you book ❑

3 a I'm afraid I can't. ❑
b I'm afraid we can't. ❑
c I'm sorry, I'm afraid it isn't. ❑
d Sorry, you are not convenient. ❑

4 a Thank you for this offer. ❑
b Thank you for your order. ❑
c Thank you, it's very well. ❑
d Thank you, that's fine. ❑

3 Wortschatz

1 For his course, Sean O'Brien needed ... from several hotels.
a delivery ❑
b offers ❑
c orders ❑
d vacancy ❑

2 He made ... with the managers of three hotels in the city.
a appointments ❑
b confirmations ❑
c stopovers ❑
d suggestions ❑

3 When they met he discussed with them the price of ... .
a accommodation ❑
b discounts ❑
c invitations ❑
d pension ❑

4 He also discussed the ... and price for a gala dinner.
a bill ❑
b menu ❑
c table manners ❑
d waiter ❑

5 ... he chose the George Hotel because it gave him the best price.
a As well ❑
b By this time ❑
c In the end ❑
d In time ❑

Business letters

1 Wie nennt man diese Teile eines Briefes? (→ SB1)

1 cc: TZ ____________________

2 Ms Ursula Heidemann ____________________
Schönlaterngasse 4
1010 Vienna
Austria

3 4 January 19— ____________________

4 Enclosures: CV, references ____________________

5 Dear Sir or Madam ____________________

6 Our ref. DL/ss ____________________

7 Regards ____________________

2 Ergänzen Sie die Tabelle. (→ SB3)

Salutation	*Close*
Dear Sir or Madam	____________________
____________________	Regards
Dear Mrs Lapp	____________________
Dear Sirs	____________________
____________________	Yours sincerely
Dear Adam	____________________

3 Josef Schwarz schreibt an eine englische Arbeitskollegin in Manchester. Schreiben Sie den Brief mit richtiger Zeichensetzung und Rechtschreibung. (→ SB5)

```
dear mary
i am writing about the meeting from 12th to 17th
november in manchester mr Lapp and i will arrive at the
airport at10.25 a.m. and want to check into our hotel
first can you plan the starting time of the meeting for
2 p.m. on 12th november thank you very much i look
forward to seeing you on the 12th
best wishes
```

josef

4 **Ergänzen Sie diese Sätze.** (→ SB Useful Phrases)

1 Thank you ________ your letter ________ 6 June, in which you asked me ___________ a meeting ________ Seattle.

2 Please let me know ________ this date suits you.

3 I refer ________ your fax ________ yesterday.

4 I would ______________ ________ if you could send the list to me.

5 ________ requested, I am enclosing the list which you asked for.

6 As I mentioned ______________ our telephone conversation, I am planning to visit Toronto ________ June.

7 Would it be possible ________ you ________ send me the list?

8 Please ________ enclosed a copy of the sales figures.

9 I ________ forward ________ talking to you again soon.

5 **Übersetzen Sie.** (→ SB Useful Phrases)

1 Ich bin jetzt in der Lage, die Fragen in Ihrem Brief vom 4. November zu beantworten.

____

2 Bitte senden Sie uns ein Angebot.

____

3 Könnten Sie uns einen Prospekt auf deutsch senden?

____

4 Ich beziehe mich auf Ihr Inserat vom 18. Juli.

____

5 Sehr geehrte Damen und Herren

____

6 Ich freue mich darauf, Sie am 5. Dezember zu sehen.

____

7 Ich möchte mich für die Kopien bedanken, die Sie geschickt haben.

____

Schlüssel

Unit 0

1 1 the 2 a 3 a 4 the 5 the 6 an 7 the 8 the 9 the 10 the

2 1 am, am 2 is 3 is, is 4 are, are 5 Are 6 is, is 7 are, are 8 Are

3 1 offices 2 salespeople 3 secretaries 4 bosses 5 saleswomen 6 meetings 7 areas

4 1 Its 2 My 3 our 4 Schaum's 5 Haas' 6 your 7 your 8 His 9 her 10 Their

5 1 Two and twenty-eight is thirty.
2 Five hundred and three hundred and two hundred is one thousand.
3 Ninety-five and four is ninety-nine.
4 Ten and five and thirteen is twenty-eight.
5 Twenty-two and fifty-five is seventy-seven.
6 Eight and seventeen and twenty-nine is fifty-four.
7 Fifteen and eleven and fourteen is forty.

6 1 It's at one o'clock/p.m. 2 It's at eleven thirty a.m. 3 It's at nine o'clock/p.m. 4 It's at ten o'clock/a.m. 5 It's at eleven o'clock/a.m. 6 in, on, at 7 to, at, on 8 at, at, on 9 on, at 10 from, at, on

7 1 February 2 June 3 May 4 August 5 October 6 July 7 November

Unit 1

1 1 F 2 T 3 F 4 F 5 T 6 F 7 F 8 T

2 1 I'm 2 'm, I'm 3 'm/am, I'm 4 is, He's 5 is, She's 6 is, is 7 'm, is 8 is, 're 9 are, They're 10 are, are

3 Fine, thanks - OK/Fine, Are - That's, Where - It's in - Are - we're

4 1 Hi/Hello, Dieter! How are you? 2 Fine, thanks. And you? 3 Ms Baumgartner, this is Uwe Heckendorn. 4 Uwe, this is Ms Baumgartner. 5 How do you do./Pleased to meet you. 6 How do you do./Pleased to meet you.

5 1 Is Sue a software expert? - Yes, she is. 2 Is this the conference room? - No, it's not/it isn't. 3 Is Richard from London? - No, he's not/he isn't. 4 Are the salesmen here? - No, they're not/they aren't. 5 Are you an English student? - Yes, I am. 6 Am I right? - No, you're not/you aren't.

6 Are you the chief engineer? Richtig. Ich bin hier für eine Sitzung mit Herrn Kaiser. Ist die Sitzung um 10.00 Uhr? Yes, at 10.00 o'clock. Und wo ist sie?/Und wo findet sie statt? Here, in this room.

7 1 Is Dieter from Hamburg? - No, he's not/he isn't. 2 Where is he from? - He's from Augsburg. 3 And Sue? Is she from Augsburg, too? - No, she's not/she isn't. She's from England. 4 Are you from Berlin? - No, we're not/aren't. 5 Are you accountants? - Yes, we are. 6 How are you? - Fine, thanks, and you? 7 Where is the meeting? - In Room 15. 8 Is the meeting at 9 a.m.? - No, it's not/it isn't. 9 When is it? - It's at 10 o'clock. 10 Who is the sales manager? 11 Are Sue and Jutta software experts? - Yes, they are. 12 Is this your computer? - No, it's not/it isn't. 13 Whose computer is this? - It's Dieter's computer. 14 Whose things are these? Are they your things? - No, they're not/they aren't.

8 1 Is this/that/it your computer?
2 Are these/those/they (y)our books?
3 Whose room is this?
4 What's the software expert's name?
5 Are you busy?

9 1 Welcome 2 free 3 How 4 Pleased 5 accountant 6 director 7 spell 8 headquarters 9 room, far 10 Where

10 their, IFC's, InfoAktuell's, Funware's, their, his, her, his/her

Unit 2

1 1 has got 2 haven't got, have got 3 has got, hasn't got 4 hasn't got, has got, hasn't got 5 hasn't got, has got 6 have got, has got

2 1 Has the company got three sales reps in Europe? How many sales reps has it got?
2 Has the Berlin branch got four telephonists? How many telephonists has it got?
3 Have they got seven technicians in Paris? How many technicians have they got?
4 Have the Berlin and Paris branches got four computer engineers? How many computer engineers have they got?

3 1 I've got an English-speaking secretary, but I haven't got a German-speaking secretary.
2 They've got a branch in Leipzig, but they haven't got a van available in Leipzig.
3 The van has got a fax, but it hasn't got a photocopier.
4 Mrs Smythe has got a big meeting, but she hasn't got a secretary.

4 1 Is there a branch in Leipzig? - Yes, there is (one). 2 Are there branches in France? - Yes, there are two. 3 Are there branches in Ireland? - No, there aren't. 4 Is there a new branch in Munich? - No, but there is one in Leipzig. 5 Are there two computers in this office? - No, there is one. 6 Is there a fax machine in this office? - Yes, there is (one).

5 1 Yes, it has. 2 No, it hasn't. 3 No, it hasn't. 4 Yes, it has. 5 Yes, they have. 6 No, they haven't. 7 Yes, they have.

6 1 to the north 2 in 3 to the west 4 to the east 5 in 6 across 7 near

7 1 staff, machines, branches 2 manager, vans, conference 3 headquarters, exhibition 4 team, available

8 1 a/one hundred and ninety 2 nine hundred and seventy 3 four hundred and fifteen 4 eight hundred and sixty-five 5 eight hundred and forty-five

Unit 3

1 1 Don't select 2 Don't press 3 Don't switch 4 Don't forget 5 Don't open 6 Don't press

2 1 Can you please close the office for the

weekend? 2 Could you please check the computers? 3 Can you please switch off the photocopier? 4 Would you please put the key in my desk? 5 Can you please tell me on Monday where it is? 6 Would you please give David the keys? 7 Can you please show me the letter? 8 Could you please give me a pen?

3 1 it 2 them 3 them 4 me, it 5 you 6 her 7 him 8 us

4 1 Do, don't 2 Does, does 3 Does, doesn't 4 Do, don't 5 Does, does 6 Do, don't

5 1 The machine works like this. 2 The machine doesn't work without power. 3 They never send originals. 4 You don't always need the overhead projector. 5 The managers never meet before 4.30.

7 she presses, she dials, she waits, she has to, she takes, files

8 2 remote control 3 calculator 4 key 5 microphone

9 1 switch on the power 2 select a page size 3 need help 4 close the door 5 press the button 6 make a phone call 7 pick up the phone 8 send a fax

Unit 4

1 1 Has Sobaku got any factories in northern England? - Yes, they have got some factories in northern England.
2 Has Sobaku got any factories in Northern Ireland? - No, they haven't got any factories in Northern Ireland.
3 Has Sobaku got any factories in the Republic of Ireland? - Yes, they have got some factories in the Republic of Ireland.
4 Does Sobaku make any small cars in Northern Ireland? - No, they don't make any small cars in Northern Ireland.
5 Does Sobaku make any estate cars in Scotland? - No, they don't make any estate cars in Scotland.
6 Does Sobaku make any cars in southern England? - No, they don't make any cars in southern England.
7 Does Sobaku make any small cars in Wales? - No, they don't make any small cars in Wales.

2 1 any 2 any 3 no 4 some 5 a 6 no 7 any 8 any 9 any 10 a 11 some 12 no 13 a 14 any 15 a

3 1 How many people are there in your office?
2 How much Spanish is there in this book?
3 How many discs are there on the desk?
4 How much salt is there in that cheese?
5 How much time have you got?
6 How much equipment is there in the van?
7 How many copies do you need?
8 How many meetings have you got next week?
9 How much paper is there in the photocopier?
10 How many working days are there before the end of the month?

4 1 a few/a lot of 2 a few 3 many/a lot of 4 a few/a lot of 5 much/a lot of 6 a little/a lot of 7 many/a lot of 8 a little/a lot of 9 much/a lot of 10 many/a lot of 11 a few/a lot of

5 1 Have you got any paper? 2 Have you got any discs? 3 How many employees have they got? 4 How many factories are there? 5 Have they got any branches in France? 6 Have you got any customers in Wyoming?

6 1 They don't produce much marmalade for the home market. 2 She's responsible for sales. 3 He handles the administration. 4 We don't use much imported fruit in this factory. 5 We fill the jars with jam. 6 These products go abroad.

7 McLaren Audio make(s)/produce(s)/sell(s) audio goods and telecommunications equipment. The company employs 800 people at its headquarters in Glasgow and its three factories in Scotland. The company sells its products in the UK and also in Europe. Ms Lethbridge is director of the sales department and has two sales managers: Ms Stewart is responsible for the UK market and Mr Bradley handles European sales.

Test 1

1 1c 2b 3b 4b 5c 6c
2 1a 2b 3d 4b 5c
3 1a 2a 3c 4a

Unit 5

1 1 Well, my room number is 923, so I think I'm on the ninth floor. 2 Well, my room number is 314, so I think I'm on the third floor. 3 Well, my room number is 511, so I think I'm on the fifth floor. 4 Well, my room number is 1202, so I think I'm on the twelfth floor. 5 Well, my room number is 131, so I think I'm on the first floor. 6 Well, my room number is 226, so I think I'm on the second floor.

2 1 Do you know if he speaks French? 2 Do you know if he's a specialist? 3 Do you know if it's with the other documents? 4 Do you know if they have got any staff available? 5 Do you know if they export to the USA? 6 Do you know if there are any meeting rooms? 7 Do you know if they understand German? 8 Do you know how many visitors there are? 9 Do you know whose disc this is? 10 Do you know where he puts the originals? 11 Do you know what the name of their text programme is? 12 Do you know how this phone works? 13 Do you know when they meet?

3 1 How much software is available for this computer? 2 What nationality is she? 3 Does this photocopier use special paper? 4 Which button do I press now? 5 How much jam do they produce in one day? 6 Where do they sell their products?

4 2 where 3 which 4 where 5 who 6 which 7 which 8 where 9 where 10 where 11 which

Schlüssel

								1							
2					O	F	F	I	C	E					
3								N	A	T	U	R	A	L	
4					F	A	C	T	O	R	Y				
5					E	X	P	E	R	T					
6					T	H	U	R	S	D	A	Y			
7	P	H	O	T	O	C	O	P	I	E	R				
8		R	E	S	T	A	U	R	A	N	T				
9					S	U	P	E	R	M	A	R	K	E	T
10							I	T	A	L	Y				
11							B	E	E	R					
								R							

5 1 one 2 one 3 ones 4 one 5 ones, ones
6 1 where 2 with 3 which 4 where 5 where 6 who 7 which 8 who 9 which 10 who
7 1 international 2 normally 3 reception 4 receptionist 5 telephone 6 telephonist 7 administration 8 management 9 restaurant 10 director
8 2 answer 3 her 4 free 5 never 6 far 7 a little 8 natural 9 dark hair 10 upstairs
9 1 It's on the ground floor. 2 It's at ten. 3 That's very kind. 4 No, it's free. 5 Yes, a little. 6 Yes, of course I have.

Unit 6

1 are flying, are leaving, are arriving, are staying, are flying, are staying, are returning
2 When are we flying from London? - At seven o'clock in the evening. - And what time are we arriving in Berlin? - At half past nine. - How long are we staying in Berlin? - Two nights. - Where are we going after Berlin? - To Zurich, on Wednesday morning. - And where are we staying on Wednesday night? - At the Hotel Metropole in Zurich. - When are we returning to London? - At two o'clock in the afternoon on the twenty-fifth.
3 1 aren't/are not going 2 aren't/are not returning 3 isn't/is not flying 4 aren't/are not staying 5 isn't/is not seeing 6 aren't/are not travelling 7 aren't/are not flying
4 In unserem Büro haben wir jetzt ein Gleitzeitsystem. Wir müssen nicht jeden Tag acht Stunden arbeiten: wir können wählen, wie viele Stunden wir arbeiten wollen. Das Büro wird um 7.30 geöffnet, aber ich muß nicht um 7.30 zur Arbeit gehen, wenn ich nicht will. Wir müssen von 10.00 Uhr morgens bis 12.00 im Büro sein, und dann wieder von 14.00 bis 16.00 Uhr nachmittags. Aber zu anderen Zeiten können wir wählen, wann wir arbeiten wollen. Ich kann an einem Tag sechs Stunden arbeiten und am nächsten Tag neun Stunden, wenn ich will.
5 1 this is 2 Can I leave a message./Can she call me back? 3 Just a moment, I'll put you through. 4 I'm afraid she's not available at the moment. 5 Can you hold?
6 1 Do you have to work tomorrow. 2 When/What time does he normally leave the office? 3 When is she coming back? 4 Do you speak French? 5 When are you seeing her? 6 Are they coming with us? 7 Do you normally come to board meetings? 8 Can I/we see the room?
7 1 in 2 at 3 at 4 on 5 on 6 - 7 at 8 to 9 to 10 - 11 in 12 to 13 past/to 14 - 15 at/for 16 to 17 on 18 to 19 on 20 of
8 1 travel agent 2 return 3 overnight 4 confirm 5 meet 6 flight

Unit 7

1 Sales of Spinn bicycles are rising/are increasing nicely. Sales in Russia are rising/are increasing dramatically. They are rising/are increasing fast in Poland, too. The market in Ukraine is rising/is increasing quickly and steadily, but the Armenian market is falling/is decreasing. The Georgian market is rising/is increasing slowly now.
2 1 Yes, he speaks English perfectly. 2 Yes, sales are rising slightly. 3 Yes, she works well. 4 Yes, our sales volume is increasing slowly. 5 Yes, our number of foreign customers is falling steadily.
3 1 perfect 2 quickly 3 perfectly 4 well 5 steadily 6 slow 7 dramatically 8 dramatic 9 well 10 quickly
4 a) 2 our visitors around the new building. 3 on the presentation 4 the new sales video. 5 the sales brochure from German into English. 6 the new building 7 for the visitors. 8 an important phone call.
b) 1 What is Caroline doing? 2 What are the visitors doing? 3 What is Mrs Campbell doing? 4 What is Steven doing? 5 What are Bob and James doing? 6 What is Tom doing? 7 What is Richard doing?
c) 1 I'm afraid she can't. She's showing our visitors around the new building at the moment. 2 I'm afraid they can't. They're working on the presentation at the moment. 3 I'm afraid he can't. He's watching the new sales video at the moment. 4 I'm afraid he can't. He's translating the sales brochure (from German into English) at the moment. 5 I'm afraid they can't. They're looking at the new building at the moment. 6 I'm afraid he can't. He's interpreting for the visitors at the moment. 7 I'm afraid she can't. She's waiting for an important phone call at the moment.
5 1 Yes, it is. 2 No, it isn't/it's not. 3 No, it isn't/it's not. 4 Yes, it is. 5 No, it isn't/it's not.
6 1 Yes, he does. 2 No, he doesn't. 3 No, they don't. 4 Yes, it does. 5 No, it doesn't. 6 No, it doesn't. 7 Yes, it does.
7 1 works, 's/is working 2 Do you know 3 's/is using 4 doesn't speak, speaks 5 aren't selling 6 do you buy 7 isn't/is not working, 's/is reading 8 don't write

8

A	B	C	I	N	C	R	E	A	S	E	A	I	B	C	D
M	B	U	N	E	M	P	L	O	Y	M	E	N	T	P	C
E	F	A	V	F	F	E	X	P	A	E	X	T	A	F	O
N	A	F	E	C	N	W	W	T	K	M	C	E	X	H	S
T	L	E	S	X	I	J	H	T	K	O	H	R	E	N	T
R	L	A	T	A	L	T	X	T	A	L	A	E	S	P	N
E	O	P	M	G	D	U	M	M	A	R	N	S	Q	E	R
S	T	Q	E	E	T	I	N	G	U	V	G	T	W	R	X
Y	Z	A	N	R	I	S	E	R	B	C	E	R	D	C	E
F	G	S	T	A	T	E	M	E	N	T	E	A	H	E	I
J	K	L	S	T	E	A	D	I	L	Y	Y	T	O	N	P
S	H	D	R	E	D	Z	Q	R	S	T	K	E	U	T	V
W	S	L	O	W	L	Y	X	Y	Z	A	B	S	C	D	E

Unit 8

1 1 higher than 2 fewer ... than 3 many ... as 4 earlier than 5 shorter than 6 longer than 7 fewer ... than 8 less

2 1 higher than 2 as long as 3 shorter than 4 lower than 5 longer than 6 as high as 7 as long as

3 1 No, working hours for teachers are as long as working hours for salespeople. No, working hours for teachers are longer than working hours for salespeople. 2 No, a modern flat in Zurich is as expensive as a modern flat in Munich. No, a modern flat in Zurich is more expensive than a modern flat in Munich. 3 No, salaries in Paris are normally as high as in Frankfurt. No, salaries in Paris are normally higher than in Frankfurt. 4 No, a job in a small town is as interesting as a job in a city. No, a job in a small town is more interesting than a job in a city.

4 short, shorter, shortest - long, longer, longest; easy, easier, easiest - difficult , more difficult most difficult; old, older, oldest - new, newer, newest; good, better, best - bad, worse, worst; low, lower, lowest - high, higher, highest; expensive, more expensive, most expensive - cheap, cheaper, cheapest

5 1 The longest 2 the shortest 3 the best 4 the longest 5 The biggest, the smallest 6 the earliest 7 the oldest

6 1 lower than, the lowest 2 the longest 3 shorter than, shortest 4 the highest, the fewest 5 the least 6 less, more 7 more, the fewest

7 1 employees 2 ATZ, salary 3 Balmar, telephone number 4 ATZ, lunch break 5 Balmar, holidays 6 ATZ, working hours per week

8 2 No, it doesn't. 3 Yes, they do. 4 No, there isn't. 5 Yes, they are. 6 No, he doesn't.

9 2 French 3 German 4 British 5 English 6 Dutch 7 Spanish 8 European
British, French, Dutch, Switzerland, German, French, German, Spanish, European, Italian

Test 2

1 1a 2c 3d 4c 5b
2 1c 2c 3c 4d
3 1a 2c 3b 4d 5c 6b

Unit 9

1 1 They think production costs will fall by £10,000. 2 They think UK interest rates will fall by 0.5%. 3 They think their market share will increase by 5%. 4 They think the pound will fall against the Deutschmark by 10 pfennigs.

2 1 Will production costs rise? - No, they won't rise. They'll fall. 2 Will interest rates go up? - No, they won't go up. They'll go down. 3 Will their market share decrease? - No, it won't decrease. It'll increase. 4 Will the pound rise against the Deutschmark? - No, it won't rise. It'll fall.

3 1 Will he be in the office tomorrow, do you think? - No, he won't. I think he'll be in London. 2 Will she be available for a meeting, do you think? - No, she won't. I think she'll be away. 3 Will the new model be more expensive, do you think? - No, it won't. I think it'll be cheaper. 4 Will they get a table at this time of day, do you think? - No, they won't. I think the restaurant will be full. 5 Will they have the meeting in Germany, do you think? - No, they won't. I think they'll have it in England.

4 2, 9, 8, 4, 1, 5, 7, 6, 10, 3

5 1 Which do you prefer, driving to the office or taking the bus? - I prefer ... 2 Which you prefer, using a blackboard or using a flipchart? - I prefer ... 3 Which do you prefer, speaking English on the phone or speaking German? - I prefer ... 4 Which do you prefer, working in your office or working at home? - I prefer ... 5 Which do you prefer, flying or taking the train? - I prefer ... 6 Which do you prefer, learning English or going out for a drink? - I prefer ...

6 1 I dislike sitting in long meetings. 2 I hate working with computers. 3 I love flying in planes. 4 I dislike eating in fast-food restaurants. 5 I like visiting foreign cities. 6 I like drinking beer. 7 I hate paying taxes. 8 I love learning English.

7 1 If production costs fall by £10,000, they'll be £130,000. 2 If interest rates fall by half a per cent, they'll be 6%. 3 If our market share increases by 5%, it'll be 25%. 4 If the pound goes down against the mark by 10 pfennigs, it'll be DM 2.45.

8 1 going 2 speak 3 be 4 to read 5 to finish 6 visiting 7 show 8 know

9

L	U	N	C	H	D	A	J	W	I	N	E
I	E	T	E	A	I	O	E	A	T	D	I
N	C	P	W	N	N	H	S	F	M	R	M
G	A	R	A	C	N	C	A	O	B	I	E
R	N	B	I	G	E	O	L	O	I	N	N
E	T	I	T	V	R	F	T	D	U	K	U
D	E	L	E	Q	W	F	F	R	U	I	T
I	E	L	R	X	T	E	K	B	E	E	R
E	N	J	A	M	D	E	S	U	G	A	R
N	F	S	M	A	R	M	A	L	A	D	E
T	R	E	S	T	A	U	R	A	N	T	Y

Schlüssel

Unit 10

1 1 Were - Yes, they were. 2 Was - Yes, he was. 3 Were - No, they weren't. 4 Was - Yes, it was. 5 Was - No, it wasn't.

2 1 Did Ian start work early? - Yes, he did. 2 Did Alison call any customers? - No, she didn't. 3 Did Alison and Jim play tennis? - Yes, they did. 4 Did Ian play tennis? - No, he didn't. 5 Did Jim and Alison work hard? - No, they didn't. 6 Did Ian work hard? - Yes, he did.

3 1 arranged 2 missed 3 faxed 4 booked 5 was 6 finished 7 checked 8 started 9 invited

4 1 I'm afraid it isn't. I have to be in London all day. 2 3.00 o'clock would be more convenient for me. 3 I'll let you know tomorrow. 4 Actually, I'd like to re-arrange the meeting. Could we meet tomorrow? 5 Yes, (that's) fine.

5 1 got 2 put 3 began 4 went 5 said 6 spoke 7 found 8 saw 9 met

6 1 They increased 2 That model didn't sell 3 Did you check 4 I didn't have 5 I spoke 6 He didn't know 7 did they arrive 8 He didn't put 9 Did she tell

7 1 will - won't 2 is - don't, didn't 3 Did, saw 4 don't, eat 5 Will - will, increase, increased 6 Is - is, sold, will 7 going/coming, go/come

8

V	I	S	I	T	C	D	L	A	T	E	F
G	A	G	E	D	A	R	T	F	O	A	L
D	L	E	A	V	E	I	R	D	B	I	Y
O	A	B	K	M	J	V	I	C	A	R	C
V	R	O	F	V	H	E	P	R	N	E	A
E	R	A	B	R	O	A	D	O	W	L	I
R	I	N	P	U	Y	Q	T	R	I	P	R
N	V	B	O	O	K	E	X	M	H	O	L
I	E	T	K	F	L	I	G	H	T	I	I
G	T	I	C	K	E	T	A	L	T	P	N
H	S	E	F	C	O	N	F	I	R	M	E
T	S	R	J	E	Q	Z	P	L	A	N	E

Unit 11

1 1 Has she put the sales figures into the computer this week? - Yes, she has. 2 Has she checked the stock list today? - No, she hasn't. 3 Has she phoned the production manager this week? - Yes, she has. 4 Has she updated the production plan today? - No, she hasn't. 5 Has she faxed the warehouse manager this week? - Yes, she has. 6 Has she updated the orders from the warehouse this week? - No, she hasn't.

2 1 It hasn't been 2 Have you spoken 3 He hasn't taken 4 They haven't eaten 5 He has gone 6 We have given 7 Have you found 8 I have written

3 1 She sold her car two days ago. 2 Have they replied to our letter yet? 3 He has never used this programme before. 4 I bought a new computer last week. - How much did it cost? 5 They have just bought a fax machine. 6 I have already seen their factory. 7 Have you ever visited their head-quarters? 8 He has found a new job for next year. 9 They changed their phone number last month.

4 1 When did you see him? 2 Did you call him back? 3 Have you called him this week? 4 How often have you been there (before)? 5 Have you been to France recently? 6 Has she finished the report (yet)? 7 Have you despatched our order (yet)? 8 Have you ever tried/drunk malt whisky?

5 receive, arrived, put, takes, haven't checked, will do, go, contact, have contacted, faxed, update, haven't updated, will update

6 1 What was the order number? 2 What quantity would you like? 3 Do we get a bulk discount? 4 I'll fax through the confirmation. 5 I'm calling about our order. 6 I'm afraid we can't deliver until next month. 7 We'll despatch it today. 8 Perhaps there's a problem with the shipping company. 9 The delivery was supposed to arrive last week.

7 (Lösungsvorschläge:) 1 How do you do? 2 Yes, of course. 3 Not at all. 4 It's on the ... floor. 5 Can I leave a message? 6 Yes, I'd love to. 7 Yes, that's fine. 8 Yes, how can I help you?

Test 3

1 1c 2a 3b 4b 5b 6d

2 1b 2c 3c 4d

3 1b 2a 3a 4b 5c

Business letters

1 1 copies 2 inside address 3 date 4 enclosures 5 salutation 6 reference 7 complimentary close

2

Dear Sir or Madam	Yours faithfully/Sincerely yours
Dear (first name)	Regards
Dear Mrs Lapp	Yours sincerely/Sincerely yours/Best wishes
Dear Sirs	Yours faithfully/Sincerely yours
Dear Mr/Mrs/Ms (surname)	Yours sincerely
Dear Adam	Best wishes/Regards/ Yours truly

3 Dear Mary
I am writing about the meeting from 12th to 17th November in Manchester.
Mr Lapp and I will arrive at the airport at 10.25 a.m. and want to check into our hotel first. Can you plan the starting time of the meeting for 2 p.m. on 12th November?
Thank you very much. I look forward to seeing you on the 12th.
Best wishes
Josef

4 1 for, of, about, in 2 if 3 to, of 4 appreciate it 5 As 6 during, in 7 for, to 8 find 9 look, to

5 1 I am now able to answer the questions in your letter of 4th November. 2 Please send us an offer. 3 Could you send us a brochure in German? 4 I refer to your advertisement of 18th July. 5 Dear Sir or Madam 6 I look forward to seeing you on 5th December. 7 I would like to thank you for the copies which you sent.